TIME
AND TIME
AGAIN

Books by Dan Jacobson

TIME
AND TIME
AGAIN

Autobiographies
by

Dan Jacobson

The Atlantic Monthly Press
BOSTON / NEW YORK

FIRST AMERICAN EDITION

LIBRARY OF CONGRESS CATALOGING-IN-PUBLICATION DATA

Jacobson, Dan.
    Time and time again.

    1. Jacobson, Dan—Biography.   2. Authors, South
African—20th century—Biography.   I. Title.
PR9369.3.J3Z477 1985   823'.912 [B] 85-47787
ISBN 0-87113-027-0

MV

PRINTED IN THE UNITED STATES OF AMERICA

CONTENTS

FOREWORD

The pieces in this volume have been called 'autobiographies' for the simplest reason. In every one of them I have tried to be as faithful to my recollections as I possibly could be. No doubt the unreliability and capriciousness of memory have led me to run together certain incidents and occasions, and to confuse some of the people involved in them. But if I have done these things, they have been done inadvertently. At no point have I deliberately departed from what I remember, or believe I remember.

At the same time, in writing the individual sections of the book I wanted not only to tell the truth, as far as I knew it, about experiences I had been through or people with whom I had been involved, but also to produce *tales*, real stories, narratives which would provoke the reader's curiosity and satisfy it; which would appear to begin naturally, develop in a surprising and persuasive manner, and come to an end no sooner or later than they should.

Obviously there is a certain tension or even a contradiction between these two sets of aims. 'Life' does not write stories. Events have no regard for narrative shapeliness. The writing of a story may often enough begin with the writer's imagination being seized by a specific person, or incident, or anecdote, or scene, or idea. But in order to give shape and meaning to what would otherwise remain a mere fragment, he has to go on to ask himself, in however rapid and half-conscious a fashion, a series of leading questions about it: 'What if – ?' or 'And then – ?' or 'Why – ?' or 'To whom – ?' Out of questions such as these, and the answers to them, which inevitably attract previously unrelated images, fantasies, and emotions, the story emerges. The form it assumes as a result of this process is frequently very different from the one originally envisaged by the writer; the germ from which the story originated may by then have been lost entirely or perhaps have become unrecognisable to anyone other than the author himself.

In this case I have asked questions like 'What if – ?' and 'And then – ?' and 'Why – ?' about some of my own memories; and have confined myself strictly to memory in trying to answer them. What I was trying to do was to turn to advantage, as a story-teller, the surprise we all feel at discovering how difficult it is to remember some aspects of our past, and how difficult it is *not* to remember others, and how little either of these kinds of difficulty has to do with our wills or wishes or even with our sense of what has been important in our lives. Nothing is more mysterious to us than the processes which suddenly present to our awareness a long-forgotten face or phrase from childhood, or which compel us to go again and again through moments we would sooner forget, or which astonish us by treasuring miscellaneous trivia, incidentals, things half-seen or half-heard, while ruthlessly blotting out the detail of scenes and events which have been of the utmost significance to us. It seemed to me that one of the advantages of writing autobiography in the episodic fashion to be found in this book is that it would preserve or even dramatise something of the erratic or fitful nature of memory, and hence something of its intensity, too. Another advantage, I was to discover, was that the individual narratives began to come together only when I let them take account of periods far longer than I would ordinarily expect a story to be able to accommodate. This was true even of those which dealt substantially with single episodes in my life or in the lives of others. In virtually every instance, my knowledge of what happened decades after such episodes, or decades before them, became an essential and explicit part of the narrative itself. Only then would it seem to be truly autonomous, self-sufficient, able to carry within itself all it needed by way of context.

The narratives do not appear in the order in which they were written. An earlier version of 'Time of Arrival' was published about twenty years ago; it has been extended and much revised for its appearance here. The same applies to 'Kimberley', which is of rather more recent date. That is the only piece in the book to have been directly commissioned – it was originally written in response to a request by the BBC for a talk about my childhood in that town – and it is also, perhaps, the least story-like among them. The remainder have been written over the last two years. The connections between them will be obvious to the reader; so will the reason why they appear in their present sequence.

In only one of the stories do I explicitly mention making a note of what happened at the time that an incident described took place. There are a couple of others which are partly dependent on more or less brief, disconnected notes of a similar kind. The rest are drawn entirely from unaided recollection. Readers will no doubt make their own guesses as to which stories, or parts of stories, fall into which category. All I can do is to advise them to be cautious in coming to conclusions.

Names (or initials) of people appearing in the stories have been altered throughout, with the obvious exception of my parents' name and my own, and that of Dr and Mrs Leavis in the memoir in which they appear.

January 1985   Dan Jacobson
London

_____ ACKNOWLEDGEMENTS _____

Acknowledgements are due to *Grand Street* ('Neighbours' and 'Last Home Holiday'); *Commentary* ('Fair Seedtime' and 'From Generation to Generation'); *The London Review of Books* ('The Boer-Lover' and 'Patient'); *Gentleman's Quarterly* ('The Calling'); *Encounter* ('The Vanishing Act'); and *The American Scholar* ('Dr Leavis').

'Kimberley' and 'Fate, Art, Love, and George' were originally broadcast on BBC Radio Three. In its revised form 'Kimberley' has appeared in *The London Magazine*.

'Time of Arrival' is a revised version of the title-piece of a collection, *Time of Arrival and Other Essays* (Weidenfeld & Nicolson Ltd, London, 1964; The Macmillan Company, New York, 1965).

'Long Weekend' was first published in *The New Yorker*, under the title 'Brian'.

PART
ONE

KIMBERLEY

When people in England or the United States hear that I grew up in Kimberley, they are sometimes vaguely impressed. 'Oh, that's the place where the diamonds come from,' they say, imagining on my behalf an exotic or exciting background. When South Africans hear that I am from Kimberley, they are not in the least impressed. 'That place,' they say. 'What a dump. I bet you were glad to get out of it.'

In South Africa Kimberley has a thoroughly bad reputation. It is supposed to be unbearably hot, which it is for a few months every year. It is supposed to be dry and dusty, which it is, for most of the year. It is, above all, supposed to be 'dead' – which it was, for many years. In the twenties and early thirties, when none of the De Beers diamond mines was being worked, it was said that a man could take a deck-chair into the middle of Dutoitspan Road, Kimberley's main street, and sit there for a morning without being disturbed. To this day the picture of Kimberley as a kind of ghost-town has persisted elsewhere in South Africa, in spite of the fact that the mines are producing again, and that in addition it has become a busy marketing and industrial centre. But the belief in its total collapse after its years of notoriety is clearly more dramatic, and hence more appealing, than the truth. There is a part of myself, too, which resists the changes in recent years that have made Kimberley so much more commonplace and conventional, by South African standards, than it used to be; which still likes to think of it as an isolated, ironic monument to the past, a symbol of a defunct imperialism and exhausted money-greed, in the middle of the silence and indifference of the veld.

About seventy miles south of Kimberley, where the road and rails cross the Orange River, you leave the truly desert-like Karroo and come to the grassveld of the Northern Cape. Instead of a sparse brown scrub, the veld is covered with pale grass and dotted with the dark tufts of camelthorn trees. Instead of rising only to abrupt stony kopjes, each one standing by itself, bearing its own litter of ironstone boulders, the veld begins to roll, to lift and fall away in great swells. In the early days of the diamond fields it was said that you could see the dust of the Kimberley diggings rising up in the air from a distance of twenty miles away; now it looks from a distance like any other South African town of medium size. Only, as you draw nearer, you see what looks like an unusually large collection of kopjes around it; when you come closer you see that these aren't kopjes at all, but mine-dumps, which surround the town like a miniature range of mountains. They are all the same blue-grey in colour; the newest are so smooth and so little overgrown they might be made of stretched silk; the oldest are so haggard and fissured it is difficult to believe that men had anything to do with forming them.

Among these dumps, and around the immense open holes from which the dumps were excavated, the town straggles. In spite of all the replanning and rebuilding which has taken place recently, it is still an irregular and confusing place. Its flat, low suburbs are pushed apart by the mines and all their debris; many of the streets of the commercial centre do not so much cross one another as lie tilted against each other. When the first diamond 'pipes' were discovered in the 1870s, people began mining feverishly before they built, and they threw down their tents and corrugated iron huts before they planned how they were going to join them in streets. So, haphazardly, the town came into being. Its suburbs were given wistfully grandiose names like Belgravia and Kenilworth. Its streets were named after people like Gladstone, Lord Milner and Lord Lyndhurst, a Colonial Secretary in late-Victorian times. The name of the town itself honoured yet another Colonial Secretary, the Earl of Kimberley, who had complained that he could neither pronounce nor spell 'Vooruitzicht', the original Dutch name of the farm on which diamonds had been found.

Monuments and statues soon began to appear. A statue of Queen Victoria was erected in a sandy, dismal park named after her; as in some old-style military cantonment, rows of small boulders marked out pathways among spindly oleander and hibiscus bushes. After the Anglo-Boer War, which he had done more than any other man to engineer, Cecil John Rhodes commissioned a bulky sandstone mausoleum to stand over the burial place of those who died during the siege of the city by the Boers. In appearance something between a Doric temple and a blockhouse, the monument bears an inscription which I managed to learn off by heart without even knowing that I was doing so, simply because I passed it so often on my way to and from school. Years later I was to discover that the inscription had been specially written at the request of Rhodes, by his friend Rudyard Kipling: *This for a charge to our children in sign of the price we paid, For the freedom that comes un-sullied to your hand: Read, revere, and uncover, for here are the victors laid, They that died for their city, being sons of the land.* Eventually Rhodes himself – child of Bishop's Stortford in Hertfordshire, graduate of Oxford, resident of Kimberley, founder of the De Beers Consolidated Mines Limited, multi-millionaire, Prime Minister of the Cape Colony, instigator of the conquest of territories which were to carry his name for seven or eight decades (Southern and Northern Rhodesia), designer of secret societies to rule the world – Rhodes himself was cast in metal, facing north, on horseback. The canvas of the original settlement had long since disappeared, but much corrugated iron remained. It still does. And more ambitious business establishments, hotels, and private houses stood two storeys high, decorated with lacy ironwork fences, gauzed verandahs, fancy gables, fretted wood. Then, abruptly, there came a slump in the diamond trade, and the town stopped growing and changing: stopped dead for a generation and more.

It was towards the end of this long period of utter stagnation that my family came to Kimberley. My father, after thirty years in South Africa, during which time he had tried his hand at a variety of occupations, from milk roundsman to soldier, from farmer to editor of a short-lived Zionist monthly, had just bought a bankrupt butter factory in the town. What brought him to Kimberley at that particular time, I now suspect, was the wish to get away from his brothers in Johannesburg, who were also in the dairy industry and who were making a greater success of their business careers than he had so far been able to do. What had brought him and my mother to South Africa in separate family groups, decades before, was a freakish movement among Lithuanian Jewry, around the turn of the century: when more Jews from that corner of the Russian empire chose to go to South Africa than to any country other than the United States. One reason why they made this choice was the spectacular success on the Johannesburg goldfields of a fellow-countryman of theirs, Sammy Marks by name.

Anyway, from the moment of our arrival in Kimberley, when my mother lifted me through the window of the train and passed me to my father, who was waiting on the platform below, my memories become clear and coherent. I was then barely four years old. Before, everything is doubtful, so much hearsay; then the sun rises on my consciousness. The image of the sunrise is a peculiarly appropriate one: for my first few months in Kimberley I seem to have kept my eyes half-closed, to escape from the sudden, surprising glare of the place. Everything glared: the sky, the iron roofs, the sand on which the town sprawled.

The contrast between the feverishness of the past and the lassitude of the present; between the self-assertion of some of the town's buildings and imperial monuments and the vacancy of earth and sky around them; between the energy and greed which had dug the open holes of the mines – thousands of feet across, thousands of feet in depth – and the air of complete uselessness and abandonment they had when I first saw them; between supposed wealth and evident forlornness; between fame and drabness – all these contrasts made a profoundly ironic impression on me as a child. It was impossible to avoid developing a sense of the tenuousness of the human settlement around me, of its dislocation, of the fortuitousness of its birth, early growth, sudden decline.

If we as a family were therefore half-alien to this scatter of buildings thrown down apparently at random on the veld, so was everyone else: alien to it and alien to one another. The Africans lived either in rooms in the back yards of their employers' houses or in sprawling, dusty, tatterdemalion 'locations'; the Cape Coloureds (people of mixed blood) lived in their parts of town; the whites in theirs. Interspersed among these groups were smaller communities: Indians and Chinese among the non-whites, Jews and Greeks among the whites. As for the major division among the whites themselves, that between English-speaking and Afrikaans-speaking, or Briton and Boer – there were very few Afrikaners in town when I was a boy, but they were still felt to be a threat by the then-dominant English. All these peoples met in the streets, they did business with one another, but just about every aspect of their social life was severely segregated. To sit together in the same room with anyone of a darker skin than their own was a moral impossibility for almost all the whites. The Afrikaner children went to Afrikaans schools; the English-speaking to English schools; the Coloureds to Coloured schools; as for the African children, most of them in those days did not go to school at all, but wandered about the streets in ragged yet timid bands. They hung about the market square, trying to earn pennies by carrying parcels for white housewives. They put their hands over garden fences or their heads into shop doorways and begged for bread or money or work. They watched us, in our 'English' schoolcaps and blazers, as we cycled or walked home from school. Beyond the wire fence around the school grounds they were the spectators of our games of cricket and rugby. One was always under the scrutiny of groups that could never finally be excluded from one's consciousness.

However none of these exclusions and disjunctions, none of the resentments, envies and despairs they visibly aroused, were permitted to put in question the quiet, seemly, orderly, small-town, petty bourgeois existence of the whites; none were felt to be incongruent with their sedate preoccupation with their jobs, their gardens, their cars, their bowls and tennis clubs, their Sunday outings, their cousinage, their gossip about one another, their exact status in the quite elaborate social hierarchy they had arranged among themselves. The highest grade in the hierarchy was that occupied by the resident De Beers directors and their connections; immediately below were the members of those families, almost all of them of Scottish extraction, who had been in business since the earliest days of the city; below them were the rest, in a definite order – lawyers and accountants, Anglican clergymen, De Beers employees, municipal officials, Jewish doctors and diamond-buyers, Afrikaner civil servants, and so on, right down to the 'poor whites', a recognised category who were held in even greater disesteem than the Cape Coloureds among whom they lived.

My parents from one world, this constrained yet half-abandoned world around me, I read in book after book of yet another: of England, of Britain, to whose empire Kimberley and the country as a whole was still supposed to belong, and because of whose empire I was being brought up to speak English and to go to a school which modelled itself as much as it dared on some vague notion of an English public school. On Saturday afternoons I went to the cinema and watched the depiction of one more never-never land: a place filled with gangsters, millionaires, skyscrapers, cowboys, Ziegfeld girls. As so many others have done, in so many varying climes, I found it wasn't the reality of the countries from which the books and movies came that I was compelled to doubt, but the reality of the country I lived in: this undescribed and un-certified place where not a single thing, from the sand underfoot to the occasional savage thunderstorm overhead, was as other places were. Everything around us was without confirmation, without background, without credentials; there was something unreliable, left out, about the whole place, and hence about all of us, too.

In school, our headmaster, an Ulster Protestant by origin, exhorted us to sing 'There'll Always Be an England', 'Hearts of Oak', and 'Rule Britannia'. The outbreak of the war, and the departure of more and more young men to the theatre of operations 'Up North', encouraged his loyalist fervour to an extraordinary degree. Then he hanged himself in the school gymnasium – not because of the reverses suffered by British arms in the first few years of the war, but because he had learned that he was suffering from an incurable cancer. In the synagogue, which I attended only intermittently and always under protest, bent men in their prayer shawls swayed in their devotions, praying in a language of which I understood virtually nothing to a God whom I seemed always to have known I did not believe in. In the factory my father owned, gumbooted Africans who towered over me were equally ready to pump up the tyres of my bicycle or to laugh boisterously at my curiosity about the work they did; later, at their leisure, crouched perhaps over one of the pots of potatoes they were always boiling in the factory yard, they would turn aside and talk to one another in languages even more impenetrable to me than that of the Hebrew prayer book, and I would know that I was the subject of their conversation and the object of their suddenly distant gaze.

How could one make sense of any of it? Well, there were many things that did not need to be understood, that could not be inter- preted, that were simply given to one. The best of these were the physical satisfactions which Kimberley offered, where the sun shone unbrokenly through entire seasons, and the uncultivated veld began practically at the doorstep of our house. On foot and on bicycles, by day and night, my brothers and I and our friends explored the town and the veld around it, finding incessant variety in the meagre streets of the one and a sense of grandeur, or of elevation at least, in the pallid perspectives of the other. We organ- ised games and races of all kinds in the lanes that ran alongside the streets, behind the houses; we indulged in some minor delinquency.

After my father had bought a cattle ranch about thirty miles out of town, we went there at weekends and during school holidays, and rode across the veld on horseback, swam and fished in the river or clambered about the rocks of its precipitous banks. The only voices we heard were our own. Over all – over intensities of light, odours of heat and drought, glittering horizons, black shadows, the stinging shriek of cicadas, camelthorn trees caught forever in gestures of alarm – rose a sky higher and wider than any I have seen since, where giant, theatrical cloudscapes were constantly assembling and dispersing. To this day the first image or form which I would give to the idea of eternity is that of the Northern Cape veld: especially perhaps at dawn, when the sun has still to rise and the prostrate earth, already paler than the sky above it, reveals once again how motionless and how untenanted are all its spaces.

If one revisits Kimberley now, one might at first glance suppose that the trance of decades ago is still on it. In fact, the town has undergone an irrevocable transformation. It is much bigger than it was. All the Cape Coloureds, almost a third of the population, have been swept off to a housing settlement so far from the centre of the city that they have given it the bitter nickname of 'Tipperary'. Where they used to live there is a new civic centre in what one might call the Afrikaner-Imperial style: slate, glass, glossy yellow and brown face-brick. Many of the elaborate Victorian and Edwardian buildings have been demolished; a few have been dismantled and painstakingly re-erected near the Big Hole, the biggest of the open mines, in a bogus 'old time' street set up for the tourist trade. The De Beers Company no longer controls the town's electricity supply, waterworks, and public transport, as it did in my childhood. One hears little English in the streets. The trenches dug by the English defenders of the city during the siege, which my brothers and I once combed through for souvenirs, have been covered over and are now the site of a drive-in cinema. At night, from miles away across the veld, one can see the imbecile blinkings and starings of its enormous screen. But no sound comes from it.

Instead a multitude of dogs suddenly raise their voices on the out-skirts of the town. One has only to listen to them for a moment to realise that their language, at least, is unchanged, and that they have nothing new to say for themselves.

NEIGHBOURS

The houses along both sides of the street were typical of those to be found in the white suburbs of Kimberley. They were single-storied and iron-roofed. They had raised cement *stoeps* or verandahs in front, and were separated from the sandy pavement by gardens and brick or iron fences. Indoors, they were divided by corridors that ran from front to back and side to side, and that met at a point where there invariably stood a hallstand or hatrack of some kind. The living rooms were in front, behind were the bedrooms, bathroom, and kitchen. Then there was a back verandah which, like the one in front, had a corrugated iron canopy over it; a yard with a few trees; and the outbuildings, servants' rooms included. The back fences of the houses were also made of overlapping corrugated iron sheets, and each fence as a whole overlapped briefly with its neighbour's. But you could always tell where one property ended and another began, since no two fences were ever exactly the same height or quite the same colour. Generally the roofs and fences were painted red or green or black. The heat of summer and the cold of winter did not make the paint blister or peel away in strips; instead it slowly became powdery, so that if you ran your hand along a fence, or clambered about on a roof, your knees and the palms of your hands came away the colour of what they had touched.

Behind the houses, on both sides of the street, there ran unpaved 'sanitary lanes'. There had been no water-borne sewerage or septic tanks in the days when the suburb had been laid out, in the first few years of the century, so buckets of 'night soil' had

had to be carted away by Africans employed by the city council to do the job. Some of the fences still had hatches cut into them, through which access could be obtained to the outhouses. Now the lanes were used for the clearance of garbage, and for the comings and goings, sittings and standings, and conversings in loud voices, of African servants and delivery men. The lanes were like shadows or parodies of the street in front, with its asphalted surface and stone kerbs and raised pavements. Undersized trees, which begrudgingly produced rough bark, thin leaves, and clusters of bitter berries in season, were planted at intervals along the pavements; these trees grew so slowly, and with such painful contortions of their trunks, that they seemed barely able to survive the heat and drought which each year never failed to bring. Yet each year, with the help of occasional visitings by the municipal water-cart, they managed it.

The street was on an incline. It was one of the handful of streets in the whole town of which this was true; the rest were quite flat. A mile or so downhill it came to an end at a high fence surrounding some mine-workings and headgear. By then it had long since lost its asphalt, its kerbstones, its trees; the houses on both sides had become smaller, shabbier, lower; they huddled together in cottage-like fashion behind scraps of gardens or no gardens at all. Unemployed poor whites and Afrikaner railwaymen lived down there. In the other direction, up the modest slope, almost every household was English-speaking. The iron roofs were decorated with false gables and turrets of wood; the gardens contained cypress trees and jacarandas, coarse lawns, bowers covered by jasmine, plumbago, or bougainvillea, and palms in large green-painted, cement pots. The householders earned their livings in grocery and shoe shops, insurance companies, doctors' and dentists' surgeries, the offices of the municipality and the mining company. They were churchgoers and members of a variety of social and sports clubs; they went once a year on holiday to the coast by train or in their cars; they employed at least one black servant who lived in a room at the back; on Friday nights they were to be seen in one of the town's two cinemas; they celebrated the weddings of their sons and daughters in the Dean's Hall or the Constance Hall, to the sound of local dance bands.

The Coneys. The household was made up of two sisters and a man who was said to be their cousin. Their house shared a fence with ours, to the side. The houses also shared, in effect, the fig and orange trees that grew in the passageways between them, since, whatever side they grew on, the trees threw their fruit and their shadows indiscriminately over the fence.

For a long time I thought the sisters were twins: they were both unusually tall, both had delicately pale complexions and long hair of an identical dark gold colour. Their eyes were blue and they often wore blue dresses. In fact there was a couple of years' difference between them. The younger worked as a cashier in a shop in town; the older as a librarian in a small, barely used, branch library down the slope. In their background was a brief, distant period of civic glory. Their father, who had owned a once-successful printing works in town, had served a term of office as mayor of the city; his name was still to be seen on the foundation stones of two or three public buildings. Long before his death, however, the printing works had gone into a decline from which it had never recovered. With their refinement of manner, softness of voice, tenderness of skin, innocence and timidity of eye, the sisters still had something of the appearance of women brought up to expect a status higher than the one they now occupied. Years later, when I was to read some of D. H. Lawrence's tales about lost or orphaned girls waiting for a young man of strong, moody disposition to awake their passions and carry them away, I was reminded of the Coney sisters. But no such young man ever came for either of them; not as long as they were our neighbours; and by the time they moved away their hair had lost its lustre and their skin its smoothness and their gaze its quality of mild anticipation. They were middle-aged by then, thickened and tired.

As for the cousin, I think he really was a family connection of some kind: in other words, the term was not merely a convenient cover or euphemism for a clandestine relationship which he might have had with one of the sisters. I say this not only because of their virginally modest appearance, but also because of the manner of the man himself. He was considerably older than they were and even more shy and retiring; so retiring, indeed, that as far as I can remember he never held a job. Or if he did, it was for short periods only. For the most part he simply pottered about the house or garden; whenever my brothers and I knocked a ball over the fence in one of our games of backyard cricket he was the one who appeared to throw it back to us; when we climbed about the trees to the side of the house, he was the one who would look at our antics from a distance. On such occasions there was a certain watchful, wistful eagerness in his demeanour, which suggested that he would have liked our exchanges with him to be longer than they actually were, and that he would have done something about it, if only he had known how. But it never happened.

Still, with his thickset shoulders, greying moustache, heavy jaw, khaki shirts, he was the man about the house. On the rare occasions when the sisters went for a drive in their car, he was the one who reversed it out of the garage into the lane. They would sit in the back while he steered the vehicle along with an air of great intensity and resolution. This showed not only in the frown of his brow but also in the fierce grip of his hands on the wheel.

In all the years the Coneys were our neighbours we never went into their house (though my brothers and I sometimes trespassed in their garden without their knowing). I can recall their coming into our house only once or twice, on inconsequential occasions. Yet in all those years we had only kindly smiles and greetings from them. We never heard their voices raised; they spoke to each other, to their cousin, to their solitary female servant, as quietly and gently as they spoke to us. They never complained about the noise we made. They rarely went out. They had no visitors. They just grew older and dimmer. Then they sold their house and went to live in Cape Town and we never heard anything of them again.

The Cleeves. They lived in one of the two houses which were directly across the street from ourselves. The two daughters of the family, Janice and Mabel (or Jans and Mabs as they were called), were about the same age as my little sister, and so they were frequent visitors to our house, just as my sister was to theirs. Both girls took after their mother: like her, they were fair-haired and had sharp brown eyes. Neither girl was fat, though, which Mrs Cleeve unquestionably was.

Her weight was just one of her problems. Her breathing was another. Her hair, which she kept short and yet constantly tormented into new arrangements of curls and waves, was another. So was the heart condition which Mabel was said to have. So, from time to time, was her husband. She complained about him to her children, to my mother, and even to my sister. She accused him of being tyrannical and tight-fisted. He had refused to have her mother in the house. He was very moody. He sometimes drank too much. He didn't show enough interest in the girls.

Her own interest and pride in the girls were limitless. The family was not Roman Catholic, but Jans and Mabs were sent to the local convent, because it was supposed to be a cut above the state school for girls, socially and educationally. They were always dressed in cotton frocks adorned with bows, yokes, pleats and straps. There were always matching ribbons in their elaborately curled and ringleted hair. Sometimes they wore matching boleros too. They had had their ears pierced when they were hardly more than infants, and thereafter their ear lobes were seldom to be seen in their naked state. They took dancing lessons (tap and ballet) for which whole sets of new costumes were frequently required, and they were encouraged to display to all their neighbours these velvet and taffeta outfits, as well as the dances for which they had been created. Mabel, the older of the two girls, had also been taught, or had taught herself, to play the piano accordion. Mrs Cleeve was never more proud than when Mabel strapped on to herself the heavy instrument, with its grinning keyboard and bellows-like, segmented body, and proceeded laboriously to press it, to pull it, to knead it, to fan it open and squeeze it shut. On summer evenings, as asphalt and brick exhaled the day's heat towards the darkening, yellow-dyed sky, a dozen or more houses might hear from her the melancholy strains of 'I'll Be Loving You' or 'Now Is the Hour'. Every note, even the most long-drawn-out, had a snort somewhere within it. My father disapproved of these performances: not because he disliked the music, but because he felt that Mabel, a girl who was said (over and over again) to have a heart condition, should not have been encouraged to undertake such exertions. His misgivings on this score were always given an air of sinister plausibility for me by the fact that Mabel was somewhat undersized for her age, and had a head too big for her body, and a chin too big for her face: as a result, whenever she heaved away at her unwieldy accordion, she looked as if she were undergoing some kind of punishment, or perhaps an obscure orthopaedic treatment.

The girls' father was physically quite different from the other members of the family. He was small and swarthy; he kept his straight black hair in place by using large amounts of oil on it, and he always wore tinted glasses, which made him look like someone permanently in the shadows. He had a clerical job in the South African Railways. Even in those days it had become unusual for any English-speaker to work for that state-owned organisation, and he used to rage against 'the Dutchies' who he claimed discriminated against him and blocked the promotion he was entitled to. This aside, one would never have known him to be the tiger and bully his wife declared him to be. When he spoke to his neighbours his manner was positively obsequious. His tight, nervous head darted this way and that, and panting laughs broke from his lips.

Still, he moved ruthlessly enough when the marriage finally broke up. First, he disappeared. Then he sued for divorce. Then he used the fact that the house was wholly owned by himself to prise Mrs Cleeve and the two girls out of it. All the tears she shed in the living rooms of her neighbours were of as little avail to her as the efforts of the lawyer she hired. She, Jans, Mabs, their dresses, the piano accordion, and much of the furniture, departed. Another family moved in. However, when I returned to the town on one of my visits as an adult – bringing with me my own children – I was astonished to find that Mr Cleeve was back in the house once again. Of all the families who had been our neighbours during my childhood he was the only one now remaining. Apparently he had never let the house out of his possession; the people who had lived in it during the interim had merely been his tenants. Now he had moved in with his new family. He had acquired a thin, trousered, no-nonsense wife, much younger than himself, who, apart from possessing a son of her own, had presented him with yet another two little girls. He looked even darker than before; his hair was thinner; his scalp was more speckled. Yet on the whole he had changed remarkably little since I had last seen him. He still wore greenish, tinted spectacles with golden frames. I never learned the names of his new daughters, and felt awkward asking him about the welfare and whereabouts of the ones I had known.

The Dalhousies. The family came from Scotland. So self-consciously Scottish a family was it that the daughters were named Ailsa and Iona (after the islands off the coast of Scotland) and the son Jamie. The two girls were almost like text-book illustrations of two different types of Scottish physique and complexion. Iona, the older, was a hefty, large-boned girl with pale brown hair and blunt features; freckles abounded on her face and forearms. Once her breasts started growing there was (as it were) no stopping them. Ailsa, by contrast, was thin, dark-haired and sharp-featured; her face was both elevated and burdened by a pale forehead and black eyebrows tilted steeply inwards to one another. Jamie was younger than the two girls. He was a victim of Down's syndrome; not so much a Scot, therefore, as a member of a nation to which only people like himself belonged. He was big for his age, and plump, and invariably wore on his close-cropped head the cap of the local high school – which he would never be able to attend.

The cap, and his girth, and the circularity of his features, and the trousers he wore pulled as high up his waist as they could go, made him look like Tweedledum or Tweedledee in Tenniel's illustrations to *Alice in Wonderland*. He smiled a great deal, and the more he smiled the more dart-like in their movement towards one another became Ailsa's brows. I would have liked to have become friendly with her, but the differences of sex and social background between us were too great for me to surmount single-handed, and she made no move in my direction. Besides, the presence of smiling Jamie intimidated me, and so did the vulnerability and severity of Ailsa's expression when she looked at him. The parents I did not know at all. The family had immigrated to South Africa just before the outbreak of the Second World War; immediately it ended they went back to Scotland.

The Redmonds. Mr Redmond was a coal merchant. He had inherited the business from his father. The coal yard was near the mine-workings, and on the far side of the railway lines that circled the town to the east. At one time he must have had four or five flat-topped delivery trucks on his routes. They were manned by powerful Zulu workers who wore empty coal sacks over their heads and shoulders, to protect themselves when they humped the full bags on their backs. Each truck had a painted wooden sign in the shape of a bow above the driver's cab. *J. Redmond & Son: Wood and Coal Merchants*, it said in curly white letters on a red background. On each side of the lettering was painted a white, daisy-like flower, viewed full face.

Mr Redmond was the only one of our neighbours who called my father by his first name. Youthful, bull-necked, dark-chinned, he had the look of an aggressive and ambitious man. His voice was loud and he stood four-square when you met him, his hands usually deep in his trouser pockets. Yet there was something lingering and uncertain in his gaze, an uneasy consciousness of self; you saw it not when he looked directly at you but when you caught him looking at others, thinking himself unobserved.

Somehow it was not entirely surprising that when voices were raised in the Redmond household, which happened quite often, it was Mrs Redmond's which was the louder, the more persistent, the one that had the last word. Then a house door would slam, a car door would slam, and Mr Redmond would drive off at speed to the nearest bar, The Halfway House, which stood about a mile away on the main road.

Mrs Redmond was shrewish in every way: in form and face (thin, long-nosed, diminutive) as well as in disposition. Of all our neighbours she was the only one who ever made an anti-Semitic remark to any of us: her chosen victim being my sister, who must have been about four years old at the time, and who had gone over to their house to play with earnest, easily alarmed Stephen, their son of the same age. 'Go away, little Jew-girl!' was what my sister, in a state of distress, reported her as saying. Mrs Redmond also tried at one time to prevent Stephen playing with the Cleeve girls. As the wife of a successful businessman and a city-councillor-in-the-making she felt it *infra dig* for her son to play with the children of a clerk on the railways. She herself, as we all knew, came from a poor family who lived near her husband's coal yard; she had been his typist before their marriage, and two of her younger brothers, both of whom walked about with their shoulders hunched up to their ears, as a way of showing how tough they were, were successively given jobs by their brother-in-law. But neither of them lasted in the firm.

Mr Redmond apologised to my father (I don't know in what terms) for his wife's behaviour, and after the lapse of just a few days Stephen was once again at the back door, looking for his playmate. However, my sister rarely, if ever, set foot in their house again.

The relationship between my father and Mr Redmond was a curious one, if only because my father showed practically no interest in him, whereas he seemed to be exercised by everything my father did and obsessed by the desire to try to go one better. What made this all the more surprising was that they were not even on visiting terms; virtually all their exchanges took place in the street or over a fence. Yet when we got a new car (a Pontiac), the Redmonds got a new car (a Chevrolet). When my father bought a farm near Piket River Station, about twenty-five miles west of town, Mr Redmond bought a farm in the same district. When my father ran (unsuccessfully) for election as a city councillor, Mr Redmond ran (successfully) for election two years later. It became something of a joke in the family, though I can remember finding it rather a disturbing one. Were grown-ups really no better than we were at school: as competitive as we were, as eager to copy one another and to show off to each other? Then what was the point of growing up? It made the prospect or process seem merely exhausting, not at all the liberation I hoped it would be.

Strangely enough, the downfall of the Redmond family followed so hard on its period of greatest success as to be virtually simultaneous with it. A year or two after Mr Redmond's elevation to the city council, with his (and her) position in the town more prominent than it had ever been, with his financial position apparently unassailable, with a new wing being built on to his house (which would have made it almost as large as ours), it was all over. He had resigned from the council, been declared a bankrupt, sold the house, was living in disgrace on the farm near Piket River, which he had prudently purchased in his wife's name. Within another year or two that was also taken from him. The problem, it was confidently said on all sides, was drink. (How much truth there was in this, I do not know. His car may often have been parked outside The Halfway House, but I never saw him drunk.) After the farm had been sold he lived on some kind of smallholding on the river, and would occasionally be seen in town, driving a battered pick-up truck, with wife, son, and younger daughter crammed into the cab, like the family of any other poor white *bywoner* or sharecropper. Then even those sightings of him ceased.

The house was bought by one of the town's Dutch Reformed congregations as a manse for its *dominee*. Though none of us saw it in this light at the time, that purchase was a clear sign of the great change which was coming over the town as a whole. During my childhood the Afrikaans-speaking element of the white population had been tiny, poor, easily disregarded, held in contempt by the English-speaking. I can remember people turning their heads in a bus to stare disapprovingly when a group of people on it had the temerity to speak Afrikaans to one another. Within a generation, however, the Afrikaners were to make up the overwhelming majority of the white population of Kimberley. This came about partly because they produced more children than the English-speaking; partly because they were in the process of migrating as a people, as a nation, from the *platteland*, or rural areas, to the cities. (And at a great distance behind them, economically, politically, socially, educationally, psychologically, the blacks were doing the same thing.)

The van der Wijzers. The *dominee* and his family were by no means the first Afrikaners to move into the neighbourhood, however. They had long been preceded by the van der Wijzers. Behind his back we had given Mr van der Wijzer the name Oom Koos (or Uncle Koos): that being a kind of generic term for any simple-minded, backveld Boer. In fact, Oom Koos was no pastoralist, and had never been one. He was a plump, loose-lipped, pipe-smoking townee, a civil servant by profession, with a skinny, would-be sophisticate of a wife who ran a ladies' hairdressing salon in town. She was the one who seemed to be full of energy and entrepreneurial ambition; he was the one who sat on his verandah in the evenings, or slowly wheeled their latest infant in its pram up and down the pavement – the very picture, in his sandals, voluminous khaki shorts, white shirt, pipe, and grey felt hat, of placidity and indolence. He always wore his hat exactly balanced on the middle of his head, with no tilt to the left or right, or to the back or front, as if simply keeping it there demanded from him a quite unusual skill.

At some time during those leisure hours of his, however, he must have read a pamphlet or advertisement telling him of the rewards awaiting him if only he invested in a few items of rudimentary machinery and set himself to work in his free time. 'An interesting hobby and a source of additional income . . .': that sort of thing. Thus it was that I was summoned one afternoon by a friend to come and see what was happening in Oom Koos's garage. Like all the other garages in the street it opened on the 'sanitary lane' at the back. Oom Koos, dressed in hat and shorts, stood in the open doorway; in front of him was a table on which were laid slabs of peanut brittle, coconut ice, fudge, and suchlike, as well as a whole battery of toffee apples, their sticks up, heads down. Behind him were some moulds and a few zinc tubs, like those used by African washerwomen, in which various kinds of confectionery were to be seen in different stages of congealment. Several other schoolboys from the neighbourhood had gathered around the garage, and a number of black servants from nearby houses, who were quite as startled and amused by the spectacle as we were. Their presence was especially discomfiting to Oom Koos. On the one hand, he wanted their money; on the other, his self-esteem suffered at the need to serve them and hence to put up with their noise and laughter, questions and pointing fingers. With a forlorn attempt at hauteur he indicated to us that he was selling his goods in this way chiefly as a favour to us; his real business, we had to understand, was with the shops and cafés in town.

My friends and I were young and easily impressed, but we had no confidence in the success of the enterprise. The garage, the lane, the sand, the clients, those washtubs, the appearance and manner of the proprietor, all told heavily against it. Still, we did our best to get what entertainment we could out of it, in subsequent weeks. We climbed over the fence to peer illicitly into the window of the garage, so that we might see Oom Koos actually practising the mysteries of his craft. We stood by when he loaded trays of his goods into the back seat of his car, for delivery to his wholesale customers. We rang at the front doorbell of the house at odd times, until he irritably forbade us to do so, to ask for a few pennies' worth of this or that item. We turned up at the appointed or official opening time ('late Thursday afternoons') when the garage door would be unfolded and he would wait for his customers to arrive. Then we got bored. Apparently the big buyers in town were also less enthusiastic than Oom Koos had hoped. After a spasm or two, the business collapsed. Oom Koos ceased to be a confectionery manufacturer. Thereafter it seemed to me that he looked with an especially baleful eye on those of us who had been his most faithful customers.

Years later, after I had graduated from university, I returned to Kimberley for what was intended to be a brief stay before I went overseas for the first time. While I was there my father fell seriously ill and was admitted to the local hospital. For many days on end, as one operation followed on another, he was either unconscious or in pain. Those were the alternatives to which his life had shrunk. The prospects of a recovery looked remote. One afternoon, in the middle of this period, I wandered into a part of the hospital I had not been in before, though I had spent much time hanging about its corridors and waiting rooms. This was a gauzed-in, wooden-floored verandah on the first floor: it looked like the kind of unused corner you might find in a grand hotel or club built, somewhere in the tropics, a century before. The gauze made the light in the verandah blurry. The air was peculiarly lifeless; it had its own trapped, dusty, metallic odour. In front of me, hardly more than a pace or two from the swing-doors I had just pushed open, I came upon Oom Koos. He sat in a wheel-chair, with a blanket over his lap. He was speechless, motionless, one eye closed, the other fixed in a stare. There was a cushion behind his head. It was obvious he had been paralysed by a stroke. So – he too was going. Everyone! To one side, on the floor, sat an African youth. His shiny brown legs, sticking out of a pair of shorts, were folded beneath him. Evidently he was Oom Koos's watcher or helper. He nodded warily at me, as if afraid I might raise an objection to his presence.

When I came back to the city after two years abroad, I found that my father had put his illness well behind him and was about to embark on yet another business enterprise. Oom Koos, however, was dead.

The Jacobsons. The family consisted of father, mother, three sons, and a daughter. My father was in business: he owned and managed a butter factory at the other end of town. It was one of the few manufacturing industries (as against service industries, or the diamond mines) of which the city could boast. My mother also worked in the business: she was its chief book-keeper. Neither had married young. They had no relations in the town. They led quiet lives socially. They seldom had guests in the house and practically never went to parties; when they did attend social functions they usually left early. Yet my father wanted to cut a figure both in the city at large and within its Jewish community. He served on the committee of the Chamber of Commerce, of the Publicity Association, of the local branch of the United Party (which at that time governed the country); he was the founder and chairman of a fund which distributed food and blankets to indigent blacks every winter; as I have already indicated, he tried once, without success, to get elected to the city council. All this was in addition to his membership of the synagogue committee, the Zionist society, and similar bodies sustained by the hundred-odd Jewish families living in the town.

My mother took no part in these activities. She had no taste for them. Paradoxically, perhaps, she had no inclination for domesticities of any kind either. She never cooked or baked or sewed or darned or knitted or gardened or arranged flowers. She did not dust or sweep. She did not even make the tea when guests came. Everything that had to be done in the house was either done by the servants, of whom there were never less than two, or not done at all. Possibly she was happiest when working in the business or when reading. Her tastes as a reader were middlebrow and middle-European: Stefan Zweig, Jacob Wasserman, Emil Ludwig, and other such forgotten worthies, enlivened from time to time by their French equivalents, like André Maurois or Romain Rolland. My father, too, was a reader, though of a different kind. He was a voracious consumer of newspapers and periodicals, taking two dailies (the local *Diamond Fields Advertiser* and one from Johannesburg); two Jewish weeklies; such journals of liberal opinion as were then published in South Africa itself (*Forum* one of these was called, *Trek* another, both long since defunct); the *Manchester Guardian Weekly* from England; *Foreign Affairs* and, later, *Commentary* from the United States . . .

To the outsider they must have seemed well enough matched, or well enough contrasted: these being so often considered the same thing, when it comes to married couples. His demeanour was assertive, even or especially when he was unsure of himself, hers retiring. He had intense, dark grey eyes and what he sometimes called 'a Habsburg lip' – that is, an aggressive, forward-thrusting lower jaw; she was bespectacled, large-headed, fine-haired, studious in expression, delicate in feature, hesitant in speech. Though his instincts were kindly, and he was always a soft touch for those in need, he was also a man of violent temper. Once his temper was lost he was quite incapable of controlling himself. His eyes would burn, his jaw would slip sideways, his voice would erupt from some otherwise dumb part of himself, he would break things, hit people with his fists, use his car as a battering ram against offending objects. When my brothers and I were young these outbursts terrified us; as we grew older we found them humiliating to witness – though I think we never quite lost a certain awe at seeing someone behave with so complete a disregard for the consequences, physical or otherwise, of his own actions.

My mother, by contrast, was gentle and undemanding in manner: she got flustered rather than irritated when she could not have her way. Given to cultivating her own vagueness in social relations, occasionally for half-conscious comic effect, she also went through spells of intense melancholia and sleeplessness which she made no attempt to explain and for which she reproached no one but herself. During such periods she would sometimes sob for long periods, quite speechlessly; even with a poignant, fugitive air of apology. I remember her trying to do up my pyjama jacket one night, and being unable to do so because she was half-blinded by tears and because her sobbing made her hands shake too much. I was old enough to do up my own buttons; but I was so upset and so filled with wonder at the spectacle that I made no move to help her.

Anyone seeing my parents together would have said that he was much the stronger of the two, and so he was in many ways; he even lived twenty-five years longer than she did. Yet in one respect she was the more truly independent and self-sufficient. He worried constantly over questions of social standing, of success, of wealth, of the proper entitlements of respect due to him and to others. He could never be comfortable with anyone wealthier than himself. My mother, on the other hand, cared as little about such matters as as any human could. It was as if she had no grasp of them, and thus did not know how to measure them. She had no wish to impress others; one perhaps unexpected consequence of this was that she was not easily impressed by the eminence of others in any field – something my father knew, and envied, and resented. Then again, while he was ill-at-ease with all his emotions, except perhaps anger, she would never deny what she felt. But how to act out of her feelings always seemed to be a puzzle to her.

The result of all this was that they got on rather badly with one another. How badly? Worse than other people? How can one of their children possibly tell? What is certain is that no one but their children, and perhaps the servants longest in their employ, knew of the strains between them. They were not the kind of people to provide their neighbours with food for gossip. (Though my father was twice formally charged in the courts with assault: once for attacking a man who he was convinced was trying to swindle him, and once, just before the war broke out, for throwing a 'Greyshirt' – i.e. a member of the local Nazi party – off the back of a truck from which he was trying to address a crowd. In the second case the charge was not pressed; the first resulted in his being fined and bound over to keep the peace.) What is also certain is that their sense of themselves as immigrants, aliens, people with a problemat-ical relationship to the land they lived in, and to the languages and cultures which struggled for dominance within it, weighed heavily

on them both. It also sustained them as a couple, since it was something they shared. This was true even though the response each
made to the unease was so different. My father was devoted to
South Africa, to its landscapes and peoples, of which he had seen
an extraordinarily wide variety during the vicissitudes of his
youth. Yet of the two of them he was the Zionist, the Jewish sur-
vivalist, the one who (though he was virtually without religious
belief) dragged his unwilling children to synagogue services and
Hebrew lessons. To have done less, especially as the Nazi madness
swept across Europe, would have seemed to him spineless, even
treacherous. To my mother, on the other hand, South Africa
seemed hardly less dreamlike than what had become of the life she
and her family had once lived in Lithuania. The word 'dream' was
often used by her to describe what she felt about the passage of
time or the relation between any one experience and another. As
for the Jews, and their history, and their survival as a group – she
simply took no interest in them. There was nothing there that she
valued. Why seek to prolong so unhappy a history? What was the
point? Better to have done with it!

Whereupon bitter exchanges would break out between them on
that very subject. He would accuse her of having no pride, of being
excessively under the influence of her atheist, Freudian, would-be
avant-garde brother in Johannesburg, of trying to turn the children
against the things he cared for; she would accuse him of being
narrow-minded, confused, the creature of his own wounded pride.
The children listened, joined in, tried sporadically to make peace
between them, and found none in their own hearts, where the
same battle was being waged in different terms, out of an experience
both the same and different.

Well, if such arguments had to take place anywhere, sun-dried,
iron-roofed, mine-pitted Kimberley, with its buildings scattered
like dark grains across the pallor of the veld, was as good a place
as any for them: as good as New York or London or Palestine
itself. That was what being in a diaspora meant. In Europe it was
too late for argument. The war broke out and the killings began.

By the time the war was over, and my older brother had returned from service in the Italian campaign, only my sister was left at home. My brothers and I went to university in Johannesburg, went to Israel, went to Europe. My father no longer interested himself in committee work: instead he threw his energies into cattle ranching, manganese mining, lucerne milling, real estate development. The years after he had supposedly retired were in fact those of his greatest financial success: a success that was much remarked on in the town, and that he savoured so keenly it could only give him an appetite for more. But my mother got little or nothing out of it. She gave up working for him; gave up finishing the books she started reading; gave up reading; gave up visiting those of her children who had settled overseas; virtually gave up walking. Then her heart gave up beating; recovered for a time; gave up utterly.

My father outlived or outstayed all his neighbours and the members of his own family too. He remained alone in the house, with a servant, for several years. He did not die in Kimberley, but at his own wish was buried in the Jewish cemetery there, alongside my mother. It was very hot when I last visited their graves: as hot as only Kimberley in the summer, in January, can be. Tall cypresses scented the air and threw black shadows straight ahead of them. The earth was parched. Many of the tombstones around bore the names of people I could remember from my childhood: each name evoked a face, or a walk, perhaps an item of clothing, a voice. All were silent now. Harvested. In the streets outside – streets too flat, too meagre, under too high a sky, for ghosts to linger in – other children were storing up for themselves memories of days, or months, or years that would seem slow in passing to no one but themselves.

FAIR
SEEDTIME

It was 'Kudu' Kemp, the master in charge of Standard Five, who set the pack on me. It was one of his specialities. A handsome, flat-faced man, he was much admired by the boys for his youth (compared with the other masters), for his suntan, for his white teeth, for his long legs, for his reputed prowess on the sports field. Even the nickname they had bestowed on him was a sign of their admiration: it referred to the fact that on some almost legendary hunting expedition he had succeeded in bringing down a kudu bull, the largest of the South African deer (which in those days had not yet come completely under the protection of the game laws). He had been photographed, like the hero of a boys' adventure book, kneeling above the beast with a rifle held aloft; subsequently he had made sure that that photograph was passed from hand to hand all over the Junior Quad of the Kimberley Boys High School.

He knew that he was popular, and why he was popular, and he played up to his popularity for all he was worth. One of the ways he did so, strangely enough, was through displays of caprice and cruelty. Thus he made sure that the white gleam of his smile, or the casual, unschoolmasterly warmth and interest he might display in his dealings with this boy or that, or with the boys in general, would be so much the more valued and competed for. Like many teachers, in other words, he behaved towards his class in a 'feminine' or coquettish fashion, as if he were some frigid, power-hungry beauty among her suitors: now bestowing a caress, now a wound; now a smile, now a frown; now a mark of concern or

even of tenderness which might suddenly be transformed into
malice. He never went too far, however, in this kind of coquetry:
he took care, that is, never to offend the boys who were themselves, in schoolboy terms, glamorous or powerful. He never tried
to humiliate them or to lower the esteem in which he knew them
to be held by the other boys. On the contrary, he sided with them
against anyone whom they had decided to persecute. We were all
aware of this, too.

There had been a couple of instances of mob savagery against
individual boys early in the year; in both cases Kemp had not
lifted a finger to help the victim. Instead he had taken the hearty,
heartless, cravenly self-protective line of accusing the victim of
being a 'sneak' and a 'cry-baby'. The first case had been that of a
new boy called Calloway who had been found guilty by the ringleaders of the mob of having 'Coloured blood'. It was also held
against him that his father's shop was in one of the poorer quarters
of the town, a district where Cape Coloureds and poor whites
lived side by side – a disgusting circumstance in the eyes of boys
whose fathers sold shoes and jackets and electrical appliances in
the city's more respectable commercial areas. What made things
even worse was that Calloway senior had a small ice-cream plant
in the back of the shop; a few pedal-driven carts with bells used
to go about the streets selling the stuff. ('Taffeta Ice Cream' was
the unfortunate trade name he used.) This ice-cream was said to
be 'dirty' and 'full of typhoid'. On several occasions I saw Calloway run like a rodent in front of a mob yelling in unison, 'Greasy
Joe! Greasy Joe!'; the pursuers in their fashion were carried as far
beside or beyond themselves as he was in his. On a couple of
other occasions I saw him trapped on a bench in a corner of the
Quad, shivering convulsively, shrinking in on himself, his eyes
hot, his face yellow and mauve in colour, while the same cry went
up and every feeble lunge he made at an escape was greeted with
a shriek of delight and a shove that sent him reeling back on the
bench. The uproar was indescribable; yet there was a sinister
silence at the heart of it, where Calloway sat trembling and the

shadows of the boys in the ring crossed and re-crossed the bench.

After many weeks of such occurrences, Calloway senior finally appeared in the school to complain about the treatment his son was receiving. Thereupon Kemp seized the opportunity to lecture the class about the virtues of 'standing up for yourself' and the contempt to be earned by those who 'ran crying home to Mama'. Much the same lecture was delivered after another boy, Louw by name, one of the few Afrikaans-speaking boys in the school, had been brought close to a nervous breakdown by his schoolmates' discovering that he had a phobia about the squat, fat, segmented, armoured, clawed, bewhiskered, thumb-sized crickets, called *koringkrieks*, which abounded in the uncleared areas of the school grounds. What better could be done with him, then, than to hold him down on the floor and put these creatures down the back of his neck, while he flailed helplessly with all his limbs, and his spine as well, and noises like those of a dog barking emerged from his chest, and tears and snot and spit flew upwards from his face?

Each time I saw anything of these torments it was simply because I had come upon them or they had come upon me. My first instinct, every time, was to clear out of the vicinity as rapidly as I could. Of course I had felt myself to be a weakling in doing so; doubly a weakling; in the first place for being utterly unable to imagine myself joining the surging, yelling, yet curiously business-like mob as they went about their work (if a score of them, or more, could do it, why did the spectacle simply make me feel sick?); and in the second place for being utterly unable, at the same time, to go to the aid of the victim – to stand up as best I could to the mob. Who knows, perhaps following either course of action, either joining the mob or defying it, might have protected me from what was to follow. But then again, perhaps neither would have.

For myself, the balance between personal advantages and disadvantages had been good enough to get me through four or five years of school without falling foul of the boys in the class who mattered most. I had never had the security of being one of the class 'bulls': I wasn't strong enough, or good enough at cricket and rugby, nor did I come from the 'right' kind of family. (Nothing very grand was involved in that last qualification: all you needed was to have a father who had been long established in business or in one of the professions in town, or who worked in any capacity, even the humblest, for the De Beers diamond mining company, or who had himself gone to the school in bygone days.) I was clever, which told against me, but was also quite good at games; I was slightly built but not 'weedy'; I was Jewish but was protected by having two older brothers in the school. During most of the year we had been under the direct care of Kemp my position had appeared in fact to be an especially good one. He liked me, I thought. He liked my essays, anyway.

Then, between one moment and the next, he turned against me; and I was done for. What happened was this. On my arrival at school one morning, I had spent some time fooling about near the bike sheds with a group of boys whom I had found there. None were from my class. They had been indulging in the ancient pastime of throwing their schoolbags at one another. Unfortunately the site of this game was near two open bins used by the caretaker to incinerate all kinds of rubbish. Rusty, capacious, triangular affairs, they were in fact two earth-moving 'pans' donated to the school by that source of all good things in Kimberley, the De Beers Corporation. Needless to say, they were caked with soot. Needless to say, once again, somebody's bag eventually fell into one of them. The game ended at that point. We stood and gazed over the rim of the bin, which came more or less up to our chests. The bag lay on an assortment of charred papers, orange peels, a few tin cans, and other such trash. At length, not because I was under any obligation to the owner of the bag, but simply because it seemed the dashing thing to do, I volunteered to climb into the bin and get the bag out. This feat was duly accomplished. None of the others seemed much impressed by it. When I came out I discovered that my hands and knees (I was wearing the school's regulation navy blue shorts) were black with soot. It was hardly surprising. I went to the lobby at the top end of the Junior Quad, where there were basins and soap and a slimy, communal towel, and did my best to wash them clean. Then the bell rang and I forgot about the whole incident.

Hours later, in the course of some lesson or other, I had to go up to Kemp's desk to get an exercise book. I had turned away from him and was walking back to my desk when he said to me in a loud, idle voice, which rang right across the room, 'Jacobson, you're absolutely filthy! Don't you ever take a bath?' Then, extending an invitation to the whole class, and making sure that it should be understood as an invitation, he asked, 'Have you seen the back of his legs? They're disgusting!' Only then did I comprehend why I had been assailed like this from behind. I looked at the back of my legs. It had never occurred to me that they too might have got filthy in my scramble in and out of the bin. But there my soot-smudged calves were, not quite as black as my knees had been, but dark enough. The boys were getting out of their desks, unrebuked by Kemp and craning their necks to gaze at the spectacle. It was a long way to my desk.

Presently the bell rang. Time for break. I was expecting to have a pretty rough time once we were released. What I was not expecting was the quasi-formal arraignment that took place immediately outside the classroom door. I walked straight into it: a group of boys waiting for me, more or less in a ring. Only two or three of them spoke, but they were the ones who counted. I remember the neatly combed hair and the utterly invulnerable, somehow aloof, expression on the face of one; the sallow complexion of another, and the eagerness or appetite he betrayed in his manner. The other boys looked on, a few of them cackling sycophantically from time to time. Why was I so filthy? Why didn't I ever take a bath? What was the big idea, coming to school like that? By dint of shoves and grabs I was made to display the back of my legs to those who hadn't yet seen them. At some point I tried to explain how it was that they had got so dirty, but this only made matters worse. Now everybody knew that I was in the habit of crawling about rubbish bins! At some other point I tried to burst out of the ring, but was hauled back into it and challenged to a fight, in the midst of all the jostling, by the biggest of the 'bulls'. Of course I wouldn't take up the challenge; then I was said to be not only dirty but 'yellow' as well.

I have no idea how long this inquisition went on. What I do know is that by the end of the day an entirely new school experience had begun for me. I had been sent to Coventry. Nobody was to talk to me or to have anything else to do with me. Everyone was to turn his back whenever I approached. At first I didn't understand what was going on – I was genuinely puzzled at the way people appeared to behave in my presence. Then I began to comprehend. Comprehension brought with it shame and incredulity, which filled not just my consciousness but my whole body, from my suddenly naked-seeming ears to the tips of my toes. What was I to do? Where was I to hide?

I couldn't believe what was happening; I couldn't believe that it was happening to me; I couldn't come to terms with the untruthfulness of what was being said about me. That my harmless, even quixotic act in jumping into that bin should have such consequences! At the same time, and in just as impacted and overwhelming a fashion, it seemed to me that I had been found out, the hidden truth about me had been made public, everything I had always known to be wrong or disgraceful about myself had at last become manifest to all. Why else should the whole community have turned against me – literally turned against me, shown me its back, moved away furtively whenever I approached and wherever I walked? To add to all this I was afraid physically, too: afraid of what lay ahead, of the lengths to which the mob might yet go.

In fact, I was spared the kind of treatment that had been meted out to Louw and Calloway; at no time was I physically hunted by the mob and brought down, so that things might be done to me when I was helpless on the ground. I did not have the assurance of knowing this, on the first day; nor, on the other hand, could I have guessed at the end of it that what I had been through was just a foretaste of what was to come, for day after day and week after week, until at last the end of term arrived. Such was the power of the 'bulls' in the class; a power which they exercised not only on me but also through me, as it were, on the class as a whole. Even now, looking back, I am amazed at the persistence with which they kept it up. There could not have been more than three or four of them who issued the orders, with a few especially eager hangers-on; but they policed their own injunction zealously and everyone fell in line, including the boys with whom I had been especially friendly beforehand.

The whole episode must have lasted about six weeks – perhaps eight at the outside – no more. If I say that I was never wholly to 'recover' from the misery I then went through, it is not because I cherish it, or wish to exaggerate it. 'What does not destroy me,' wrote Nietzsche, in tensely self-consoling style, 'makes me stronger.' Well, no one is a *tabula rasa* at the age of eleven, and all that was strengthened in me were certain pre-existing tendencies and patterns of response, most of them of a pretty negative kind: self-doubts (hardly what Nietzsche would have had in mind); a susceptibility to the notion that people will always be ready to gang up on me, if given the opportunity to do so; scepticism about my own motives and everyone else's; a kind of primitive but thoroughgoing scorn for those who speak in their books or prayers or speeches as if some mass transformation of the human will or of human institutions might one day produce a race nobler or purer than the one we have – or are. The episode often came into my mind in later years when I speculated about how it could have been possible for incomparably greater horrors to take place: about the ever-repeated psychological manoeuvres which had to be gone through in innumerable, individual minds before the Nazis could put into effect their intention to slaughter the Jews of Europe (a programme which began in the very year that the events I am describing took place); and about why the Jews reacted as they did to what was happening to them; and about why those who were neither Nazis nor Jews reacted, or failed to react, as they did. The same was true for the way in which I was to think about some aspects of race relations in South Africa; or about the impulses that make the victims of a hijacking speak so effusively not of their rescuers but of the people who kidnap them and brandish guns under their noses for days on end ... and so on. Of course it isn't just 'them' and what 'they' did whom I think of in such contexts, but myself and everything I did. The latter even more, perhaps, since I know it better than the other.

Among some minor, additional lessons I learned then (if I had not known it before) was that an enforced isolation could be almost as varied in its tones and modes as happiness or companionship. This did not make it any the less intolerable. There was, for example, the loneliness I experienced when I was sitting in my desk in the classroom, which was different from that which I experienced outside the classroom, which in turn was different from what I experienced at home. There I was safe from my classmates and from what they could do to me, but my own determination to say nothing of what I was going through effectively isolated me from my parents and my brothers. Inevitably, I courted some forms of loneliness, precisely so that I could think of them as arising from my own choice, different in some tenuous fashion from the isolation which was being inflicted as a punishment on me. The moment school was let out I raced off home on my bicycle: that way I had the consolation of avoiding being avoided by the others. I would also avoid the possibility of those who were *not* my classmates seeing how I was being treated by them, and perhaps being moved to follow suit. The same applied to my journeys to school: if I wasn't with one of my brothers I would dawdle deliberately when I saw anyone from my class ahead of me on the road; or I would cycle up the dusty 'sanitary' lanes that ran behind the town's residential streets, in order not to see the others or to be seen by them.

Since I was being treated like a criminal, in other words, I began to behave like a criminal: I became furtive, secretive, a holder back of the truth even from those at home whose goodwill towards me I never doubted. I also turned into something resembling an invalid – and this not only because I used every sniffle that affected me, every sprain or graze, to plead to be let off school, and would lie in bed night after night, fervently hoping to wake the next morning with a temperature or a rash. No, I was like an invalid in the sense that I could take none of my movements for granted; all the cunning and caution I could summon up had to go into carrying out the most trivial tasks; everything I did exhausted me. Indeed, one of the clearest memories I have of the whole episode is the effort that was constantly demanded of me: the effort of silence on the one hand, and the effort of speech on the other; the effort of driving myself to school each morning and of getting through the rest of the day; the effort of having to think out my moves several stages ahead in order to outwit my persecutors. Not to speak of the effort of meeting their stares or not meeting them; of noticing or pretending not to notice their movements away from me; of pretending, while the lessons lasted, that I was a schoolboy like any other; of looking for a place in the mercilessly naked school grounds where I could eat my sandwiches without my solitariness becoming manifest to all.

In some ways conditions were easiest for me when we were all gathered together in the classroom, participating in the lessons, forbidden to talk to one another; then, I used to think, no one looking at us could have told me apart from the others. For the first and last time in my school life I wanted the lessons to go on longer; I hated the sound of the school bell telling us that it was time for one of the two breaks we had; even the sound of the bell at the end of the day did not really bring relief, since it meant that I now had to negotiate the passage between home and school. Of course at no time did I speak to Kemp of what I was going through. He was responsible for it, first of all, and I knew that I could expect nothing from him in the way of help or contrition. Besides, the looks I sometimes caught from him made me suspect strongly that he had a pretty good idea of what was going on. He would never give me the satisfaction, however, of knowing for sure, one way or the other.

At home I preserved my silence simply because I did not want to acknowledge to my family what a miserable pariah and failure I was. No consolation that might have been forthcoming from them would have made up for the pain of admitting to them the condition I was in, or of having to turn to them for succour. Thus, at home as well as at school, I learned how close to one another are certain emotions which we ordinarily like to think of as being remote from one another, if not to all intents and purposes mutually exclusive. Shame, I discovered, could be indistinguishable at its roots from pride, and vice-versa; the same was true of weakness and a certain kind of stoic reserve or silence. Entrapped within the meshes of emotions like these there lurked also the fear that if my parents did hear of what was happening at school, and of the part Kemp had played in it, they would have complained to the headmaster or, if they had not got satisfaction from him, to the governing body of the school. I could not face the thought of it, of any of it: the gossip, the enquiries, the whole school learning of my humiliation, Kemp lecturing me about cry-babies, or, for that matter, Kemp being lectured at by people more powerful than himself, and thereafter bearing an even bigger grudge against me than before. In a peculiar fashion, therefore, I actually felt protective of him; not because I wished him well, but because by protecting him I would be protecting my own feelings from the laceration of further exposure.

Kemp was not the only one I protected in order to protect myself. I did the same with some of the boys. This applied especially perhaps to those whom I knew to be unhappy about what was going on, and who would have spoken to me or befriended me if only they had dared. Sometimes it seemed to me worse to find myself among the more kindhearted of the boys than among the relatively few who enjoyed what they were doing to me, and did it with conviction, with relish, out of an evident belief that in chastising me for being dirty they were certifying themselves as clean, upright, fully accredited members of the community. There was no comfort – quite the reverse – in seeing the meek, secretive gestures of goodwill sometimes made to me by the other boys, or the mute guilt in the eyes of those who had been my companions prior to my banishment. If that was as much as they could offer me, if they would speak to me in embarrassed, hesitant fashion only when they knew themselves to be safe from spying eyes, then how alone I really was! Besides, in their looks I could read not merely the shame they felt at their own thoroughly cowed state, but also the fear that I might betray them subsequently by claiming their friendship in public, and thus revealing them to the others as secret backsliders. I did not want to put them through it; still less did I wish to be reminded that all I was for them was an object of furtive pity and an occasion of misgiving. There are boys whose names I have long forgotten but whose sidelong, shamefaced glances, whose stiffened cheeks and pained brows and awkward shoulders, I can still remember vividly; I can remember also the particular places in the school grounds or outside it where such glances came my way, and the spots of sunshine on the inner verandah of the Quad, or the sound of bicycle wheels on a tarred road, that accompanied them.

One surprising feature of the whole performance – more surprising perhaps in retrospect than at the time – was that at no point, so far as I can remember, did it take an anti-Semitic turn. That much must be said to the credit of my persecutors. The fact is especially noteworthy since there were in the school some boys who, at the age of ten or twelve or fourteen, were already accomplished, not to say obsessive, anti-Semites. (All this took place in the second year of the World War, and to the inevitable or 'endemic' anti-Semitism which might be expected anywhere and at any time, and especially in a country as racially inflamed as South Africa, there had to be added the effects of years of Nazi propaganda.) Such boys were eaten up by their preoccupation with the Jews, maddened by it, perhaps even – it would be consoling to think – tormented by it, and by their inability to do anything with it other than shout insults at the Jewish boys. Fortunately for me there were none of them in my class. One other interesting circumstance is that so far as I can recall no boys from other classes were ever called on to take part in the boycott; it was as if the class 'bulls' were not going to endanger their power by trying to stretch it too thin. In that respect they proved themselves to be cunning tacticians.

It would be gratifying to my own sense of the dramatic to be able to record that some single act of rebellion on my part or of compunction on the part of my persecutors brought the episode to an end. The trouble is, it would be quite untrue. Nothing of the kind occurred. All that happened was that the term came to an end. For six weeks school ceased to exist; a period which was in itself about as long as my persecution had endured, and which, like it, I perceived almost as if it were a realm of its own, without antecedent or limit. This way of apprehending time seems to come naturally in childhood; we recover it as adults only during passages of illness or other forms of extreme stress.

Nevertheless, when school reassembled, as it inevitably did, I went back to it with much anxiety. We were going to go into a new class and we were to have a new teacher; but I did not know how much difference that would make. What I did know was that I would not be able to endure a renewal of the experience I had been through. If it did all start up again, I would have to act in some way; how, I did not dare to imagine.

In the event my misgivings turned out to have been unwarranted. Nothing happened. Nothing at all. The whole episode had been forgotten by everybody other than myself. Or so it seemed. The boys who had set the class on me greeted me neither with hostility nor with any air of apology. No one accused me of being dirty. As arbitrarily, as nonsensically, as the persecution had begun, it had ceased. A recollection of the blank, anti-climatic arbitrariness of it was to return to me when I set foot on the continent of Europe for the first time, at the age of twenty, knowing that had I been in that very place five years previously I would have been a hunted man, someone condemned to death. Now I was not. The ban had been lifted. That was all there was to it. One thing, though, about myself at the age of eleven which must not go unmentioned was the impulse of craven *gratitude* I felt towards the ringleaders of the mob when I realised that I had indeed been 'forgiven'. I can remember sitting in my desk and feeling it go through me like a flush. They liked me! How generous they were! How kind it was of them to re-admit me to the class! Then came a flush of another kind, as I realised why I was feeling grateful, and to whom.

As for 'Kudu' Kemp, the ultimate begetter of the experience I had been through, he left the school to go into the army in the course of that year. He received a commission in an infantry regiment, fought in North Africa, was captured by the Germans, escaped from them in circumstances that won him a decoration for gallantry, and returned to the town at the war's end as something of a hero. Two years later, though he was then still only in his mid-thirties, he died of a heart attack.

THE
BOER-LOVER

Like all the older people among my mother's family connections, N was an immigrant to South Africa from Eastern Europe. He had arrived in the country as a boy and had grown up in Johannesburg. Unlike virtually every other Jewish immigrant, however, he had subsequently chosen to identify himself not with the urban, prosperous, relatively sophisticated English-speaking section of the population, but with the Afrikaners. As a group they may have had the reputation, at least among outsiders, of being provincial, defiantly racialistic, isolated from the rest of the world as much by their attitudes and language as by their geographical situation. Indeed, when my two older brothers and I lived briefly under N's roof, more than forty years ago, a substantial number of the Afrikaners sided more or less openly with the Nazis in Germany. Yet it was with them that he sought to associate himself; it was with their fortunes that he had tied his own. Tied it to the extent of marrying an Afrikaner woman and bringing up his children to speak Afrikaans. For years his mother had refused to see him, as a result.

That was one remarkable fact about him. Another, closely connected with it, I shall come to presently. At that time, no doubt as part of his programme of 'going Boer', N had bought and was running a substantial farm in the very middle of the flat, treeless, landlocked, middlemost province of the country. One summer it was decided that my brothers and I should spend our school holidays there. This would solve the summer holiday problem quite cheaply; besides, my father, who had himself been a shopkeeper and a small-scale farmer in that part of the world, had a sentimental attachment to it, which he wanted us to share. As for N, I suspect that he was lonely and bored and that he welcomed the idea of company of the kind (our kind) on which he had supposedly turned his back. Even if, as in this case, it was under age.

In the event, the holiday was not a success. We lived on the farm for about two weeks, no more; but it seemed longer to us, as it must have done, I am sure, to our hosts too. We got on badly with N's two children, who were younger than ourselves, and neither badly nor well with N's wife, who was too reclusive to have any relationship with us, apart from that involved in silently ladling out soup at the dinner table. When I say that N had married an Afrikaner woman, I don't want the reader to picture to himself some sturdy, bonneted *Boerevrou*, dressed in calico prints on weekdays and in church-going black on Sundays, given to sausage-making and child-bearing. Nothing of the kind. N's wife was an elongated, indoors person, who invariably powdered her face so thickly as to produce a mask-like or plaster-of-paris effect, which was relieved by a strongly lipsticked mouth and a pair of tinted glasses. Her hair, gold-foil blond in colour, always looked as if it had been freshly dyed and permed; her shoes, stockings, and dresses were always formal and fashionable. Having carefully rigged herself out in this manner each morning, like no other farmer's wife in the province (I should guess), she would proceed to spend much of the day behind drawn curtains in the bedroom. What she did for all those hours in her room I have no way of knowing, or even of guessing. Only years later did it occur to me that perhaps it was our presence that had driven her to take refuge there. She would emerge for meals, which were prepared by the African women in the kitchen, or to spend some time with her children in the afternoons; then retire early to bed. Whenever she went out, the occasion seemed to be fraught with an intense but obscure sense of risk.

N, by contrast, was always on the go. Even when he sat down he managed to remain on the go. His voice was loud and hoarse, his gestures were emphatic, his laugh came readily and lasted for a long time, he was always eager to engage the whole of himself – shoulders and hands as much as mind – in passionate argument. Having thrown in his lot with the Afrikaners, having decided that their fortunes were to be his, he had adopted the attitudes which he felt to be appropriate to his choice: he had schooled himself to despise all liberals, left-wingers, reformers, bleeding-hearts, 'kaffir-lovers' and suchlike. During that holiday he tried to get us to do likewise. Thinking of him then, of the vitality that was in him, I do not find it hard to bring together the dishevelled gregariousness of his manner with the views he put forward. It is more difficult to reconcile his manner with the knowledge that his entire life was spent in flight from one kind of isolation and in pursuit of another, until, as we shall see, he could bear neither any longer. Even on the farm there was distance enough between him and his wife, not to speak of the distance between him and his two sons: a solemn pair of children with cropped, sun-bleached hair and sun-browned legs, who did not like our being there and who showed a wincing unease at the copious (and to them largely incomprehensible) draughts of English with which N regaled us – and himself. 'Chaps' was the hearty term he invariably used in addressing us; a word which his children had evidently never heard before. His repeated use of it eventually moved the younger of them to say to us one day, in a tone of disgusted bewilderment, '*Julle kêrels is net'n hele klomp chaps!*' – You blokes are nothing but a whole bunch of chaps!

That was the family. The house was a smallish, newish, box-like affair. Parked on a slight rise, it looked across wide fields and grazing lands and over a muddy river towards other farmhouses on similar rises, each one with its accompanying clump of trees. Then came the horizon, which was as firm as the rim of a bowl resting on a table. My brothers and I went for walks across this landscape; we tried swimming in the river; we watched the African farmhands milking the cows and had a go at it ourselves (how wholly unexpected, and how shamefully erotic, was the sensation of grasping the cow's teat between thumb and fingers for the first time); sometimes we accompanied N on the expeditions he was continually making in his car to various points in the neighbourhood. Most of these expeditions were of no importance; they were merely an expression of his restlessness, a way of passing the time.

Often enough he used to go to the nearest *dorp*, a place called Driekop which had the attractions of several shops and a railway station. Driekop was both small and sprawling, with wide, unpaved roadways and lots of grassy spaces between its buildings. Only the spire of the Dutch Reformed Church rose above single storey height; only the church was roofed in slate, not corrugated iron. The windows of the general stores were given over to a jumble of articles; other windows were devoted to one thing only – agricultural machinery, say, or coffins and funeral draperies. At the end of every half-formed street was the green surge of the veld, forever about to engulf the place, or a dirt road heading between two wire fences for the horizon. From place to place, amid these exiguous surroundings, N bustled about: a slight, red-faced man with a gleaming eye. His elbows stood out on either side of him, like handles on a vase, while his abbreviated legs bounded along below. The locals, most of whom looked as though they weighed about twice as much as he did, evidently thought of him as an oddity; but they did not do so, so far as I could see, with any affection. Affection did not come readily to them. N was not to be daunted, however. 'Come on chaps,' he would call to us, and we, having nothing else to do, would slouch along behind him, acutely aware of ourselves as aliens in this dourly Afrikaans-speaking, nationalist-voting landscape.

Perhaps my most vivid, single memory of the visit as a whole, however, is of the time I spent on the farm following the plough. The work was still being done in traditional style, with a team of four oxen pulling the plough, and two men following it, one with a long whip which he would crack over the beasts' backs, and another who held the handles of the plough and steered it along, and disengaged it at the end of each furrow, where the oxen would turn to begin the next. In front was the jangling, snorting, stumbling, sweating team with the whip cracking repeatedly over the toss of their heads, the heave of their haunches, the bunching of their shoulders and the splay of their feet; everything there was noise and effort and harnessed will. Behind all this, and beneath it, with an astonishing sleekness and silence, with an effortless simplicity, the tip of the plough cut through the earth and turned to one side a black, moist roll of soil which screwed away from the blade that had created it in one overflowing, never ending turn. I have only once seen since a paring or cleaving movement that had so sustained an air of hypnotic ease to it: many years later I was to cross the Mediterranean on a boat small enough and ill-organised enough to permit me to lie at the most forward point of the deck and look down (look behind, actually) at the prow cutting the water some feet below. There the motion produced a transparent pair of water-wings travelling at one height above the darkness of the sea; but the ease of the motion and the hiss which accompanied it took me back at once to the plough cutting the fields of N's farm near Driekop.

Then, rather sooner than had been arranged originally, we left the farm to go home. Ostensibly this was because some of N's in-laws were coming unexpectedly on a visit over the holidays. Perhaps they were. I do know, though, that the day before the change of plan, our relations with N's children had reached their lowest point. For this I was in large part to blame. We had been wrangling over something or other in the yard immediately behind the house. One of the children made a remark that irritated me particularly. Without thinking what I was doing, I kicked towards him the dog's feeding bowl which happened to be right at my feet. What I did not know, or took too little notice of, was that there was about an inch of milk still in it. The bowl skidded along the path for a moment, before it struck against a pebble. A sheet of milk, with a fringe of drops hanging from the end of it, like lace at the end of a petticoat, flew into the air. The little boy, my host's son, received it full in the face and chest. He fled howling into the house.

Our visit was over. Whereas N had taken the trouble to meet us at Bethlehem, the nearest rail junction, when we had arrived, we were put on a local train at Driekop for our departure. We were to change trains at Bethlehem in order to make our way to Bloemfontein, where we would change trains once again to get to Kimberley. How precipitate our departure was can be gauged from the fact that it was on Christmas Day itself that we left for Bethlehem. The empty, idle journey we made that day may seem to have nothing to do with our dealings with N; his sole connection with it was to see us on to the train, and to be seen by us as a solitary, waving figure on the receding platform of Driekop station. For me, though, it is as if everything that came our way after he had fallen out of sight, even the freakishness of our travelling to a place called Bethlehem on that particular day of the year, belongs to him as much as does anything else that happened on that holiday. Even at the time it all somehow seemed to be an expression or projection of the circumstances he had arranged around himself; or, to put it more grandly, of the singular destiny he had chosen for himself.

The little train to Bethlehem was virtually empty. There could not have been more than a dozen people in the three or four coaches of which the train was made up; they all appeared to be white, male, and Afrikaans-speaking; many of them were drunk. (The segregated third-class coach at the front of the train, where it would catch the smuts from the steam engine, was empty; the blacks were evidently lying low that day.) It wasn't only some of the passengers who were drunk, but also the staff, engine-driver and stoker included. As far as the latter two were concerned, we learned this when the train drew up at the first stop after Driekop. It was nothing more than a nameless siding, with a cattle pen to one side and a shed to the other, and not a soul stirring in the expanse that lay around it; yet for some reason the train waited there, engine fuming, for about thirty minutes. During this time the stoker and driver left their cab and joined the guard and ticket inspector for an impromptu party, together with a couple of the passengers. Leaning against the railings of the cattle pen, they spoke noisily among themselves, laughed, handed around a bottle, smoked cigarettes. Then the journey continued. The same scene was repeated a few stops later. Shortly afterwards, while the train was still in its ambling or trundling motion, the stoker emerged from the cab of the locomotive and clambered on to a narrow, unrailed platform or gangway that ran alongside the boiler. He made his way along this gangway, trailing behind him a single coloured streamer of crinkly paper, of the kind people hang from the ceiling of shops or houses on festive occasions. Somehow or other he managed to suspend that frail decoration along the barrel of the engine, while the wheels and pistons continued their ponderous work below. Then he did the same thing on the other side. At the next stop we went to the front of the train to admire the effect. The streamers looked both gallant and pathetic against the engine, let alone the vacant countryside, and the incomparably vaster sky overhead, where, in the remote distance, some stormclouds were gathering. It was as if the elaborate geography of an alternative continent, complete with lakes, shores, mountains, and plains, was silently being assembled up there.

The engine, which had long since lost its streamers, pulled us into Bethlehem station towards midday. Bigger than Driekop, Bethlehem had tarred streets, many shops with concrete porticoes sticking out above the pavements, two or three Dutch Reformed churches, and a rather ambitious main square, where lawns and beds of flowers surrounded a new town hall. The shops were all closed, the churches deserted (services were evidently over for the day), the streets quite empty, the town hall locked. We had it all, stark sunshine and shadow included, to ourselves. Everyone was at home for dinner, it seemed. The blacks were safely confined to their 'location', a mile or so out of town, which we had seen from the train. Eventually we found on a corner a shop-cum-café, run by a couple of young Greeks, which was open. We were not the only ones to have taken refuge there. In addition to the shop-keepers behind the counter, there were three soberly-suited but boisterous men in front of it. They had apparently been there for some time. None of them seemed to have bought anything. They greeted our arrival with a lot of indeterminate noise. One of them drew my oldest brother aside. He opened his jacket. Nestled in the inside pocket, like a small pet a child might carry about with him, was a bottle of Cape brandy. He unscrewed the top of the bottle while it was still in his pocket and made as if to pour out its contents simply by tilting himself forward at an acute angle. 'Go on! Have a drink!' he shouted at my brother in Afrikaans. He wagged a finger at my remaining brother and myself. 'You're just kids. You drink lemonade, hey. But this *outjie*' – lurching again at my brother – 'he drinks brandy!'

Through an archway to one side of the shop we could see some chairs and glass-topped tables; on each was a menu card stuck into a holder. But no meals were being served. There was nothing doing in the kitchen, we were told, because all the 'boys' were gone for the holiday. All we could have was a cup of tea and some biscuits, or a soft drink. In the end we had our lunch, consisting of a bottle of fizzy orange apiece and a shared packet of biscuits, *al fresco*, sitting on the granite steps of the town hall. Once the three men who had been in the shop had departed, after some skirmishing among themselves on the pavement, and a howitzer-like banging of the doors of the car they got into, nothing disturbed the early afternoon stillness.

Our meal had long been completed when four or five boys on bicycles appeared. They must have been let out of their homes to find what amusement they could by riding around the empty streets of the town. They were somewhat younger, on the average, than ourselves. Like flies in a room, they zig-zagged pretty much at random around the square. When they spotted us, however, their curiosity was at once aroused. They could not really get close to us on their bikes, because the town hall and its gardens were separated from the road by a whole series of obstacles: a low wall, steps, ornamental chains. But they were unwilling, or perhaps afraid, to approach on foot. So they circled about, as near as they could, first from one side, then from the other. At last their scrutiny of us produced the clarification they were looking for. '*Jode!*' they shouted, by way of insult to us and explanation to one another. '*Jode!*' Now they knew what kind of an animal these strangers were. Now it was clear to them why we should have been sitting in the middle of Bethlehem town square, on Christmas Day, with no home to go to, no dinner in our bellies, no friends to visit. Having uttered these cries, being satisfied with what they had learned and what they had done about it, they rode away in search of other entertainment. We returned the empty bottles to the café and began retracing our steps towards the station. Only another hour or so to go before we could resume our journey. We would have to go through another wait, even longer than the one we had just endured, when we changed trains in Bloemfontein.

All this I remembered when I heard, decades later, of N's death; and of why and how he had come by it. After that holiday I saw him no more than half-a-dozen times, perhaps, in all. At least on two of those occasions it was in London that we met. I had settled in London; he had come there to try to find a market for an industrial mineral of which a deposit had been found on his farm in Driekop, and which, characteristically enough, he had at once started to mine. He was long since divorced by then, and had never remarried. I gathered that his relations with his grown-up sons were difficult: he had quarrelled with the bride which one of them had just acquired, and he disapproved of the other's choice of profession. He was at pains to tell me that he didn't think much of the fiction I had published about South Africa: according to him I did not know enough about 'the real South Africa', on which subject, after his years in Driekop, he obviously felt himself to be an authority. On his second trip to London he actually succeeded in getting a well-known merchant bank to invest a substantial sum in his mining operation. Thus those fields I had watched being ploughed became a matter of concern in a City boardroom. There was even an article about him in one of the Sunday papers.

The business fizzled out eventually; but that failure was not what led him to take his life some years later. No, it was the presence of Cuban troops in Angola. (Here, like any other writer of fiction who tries to tell the truth I have to say, perhaps unavailingly, that this *is* the truth: I would not have dared to invent such a tale.) The Afrikaners' success in taking over South Africa and running it as they pleased, and not as the English-speaking might have liked, let alone the blacks and their overseas friends, he had always seen as a vindication of a central choice, or series of choices, he had made, and as a crushing defeat of those who had pitied his perversity, shaken their heads over his marriage, condescended to his views. And then, after he had proclaimed those views and lived by them for so many years, what had happened? The Cubans had appeared in Angola! The Communists were about to march in! Afrikanerdom (in his by then diseased imagination) confronted its ultimate enemy. How could the strength of the Afrikaners, which may have been sufficient to oust the English-speaking from their position of political supremacy, and to keep the blacks in their place, be compared with that of a superpower like the Soviet Union, of whom the Cubans were the mere surrogates or advance-guard? The Afrikaners had suddenly become history's losers, it seemed to him, not its winners. Perhaps, in the pitiless eye of history, he had made the wrong choice, after all.

So he shot himself. First he shot his dog, who by that time was his only trustworthy companion; then he turned his pistol on himself. No doubt the obsessive melancholy and dread which had focused itself so improbably on the Cubans in Angola would have found something else to dwell upon if no Cuban soldier had ever set foot on African soil; but still, that was the reason he gave for his deed; that was the form his final mania took; and it cast its own light on everything that had gone before.

These recollections included. I am sure that of those boys who rode their bikes around us in Bethlehem not one has been moved to take his life because of the threat to the Afrikaner people posed by the Cubans in Angola. But then, it must be said of N that he had always had the courage of his own desperations.

THE
CALLING

Chemise.

It was that one word, the pronunciation of which differed so mysteriously, to my ears, from its written appearance, that made me fully conscious of just how much I wanted to be a writer. More: it made me feel as if I had already become a writer. It had happened. The decision had been made. Now all I had to do was the writing.

She-mēz.

Of course the idea of 'being a writer' had long attracted me, even though I could not have said what I meant by the phrase. An ace reporter, in a hat, like those I saw in the movies on a Saturday afternoon, seemed to me as much a writer, and as much to be admired, as someone producing novels like Aldous Huxley's, full of what I took to be devastatingly erudite and cynical conversations. The same was true of poets like John Keats or Alfred Tennyson, who wrote lines about the murmurous haunts of flies on summer eves, or about a wind that shrills all night in a land where no one goes or has been since the making of the world. Also, as far back as I could remember I had been in the habit of mentally transcribing much of what I saw and did into words – any words, boring words often enough, words which I would sometimes silently foist on to the minds of other people, someone I might pass in the street for instance, who would be made to describe what *he* saw, and would thus unwittingly be pressed into the service of my compulsion. And that compulsion, too, I thought of as a kind of 'writing'.

So in a sense I was ready enough for what happened to me in

the course of an English lesson during one of my last years at Kimberley Boys High School. Yet it is precisely those changes for which we are inwardly prepared that sometimes come upon us with an effect of great surprise. If we were conscious that we were waiting for them, they might never come; if we had an inkling of the form they would assume, they would change nothing.

Chemise.

As a class we were engaged in a reading of *Eothen* by A. W. Kinglake. For reasons hard to imagine, someone in the Cape Province Education Department had decided that this Victorian gentleman's account of his travels in the Levant would be an appropriate set-text for our matriculation examination in English Literature. On that afternoon we were being read to in soft, clear, self-assured tones by our English master, 'Dainty' Manders. Sitting in a chair in front of the class, he gave full value to all the implications – condescending ones, mostly – of Kinglake's prose. Because it was a hot afternoon he had taken off his jacket to reveal a cream, short-sleeved shirt. His silver hair was sleekly combed away from his forehead. His skin, as always, was beautifully shaven; the pores were there, but never the hairs that might have appeared within them, at that hour, on another face. The Kimberley sun seemed powerless to dry out his complexion, or darken it, or make it sallow. Instead it kept its pinkness and silveriness, and somehow managed to transform these into a transparence as well. His eyebrows had remained, or were carefully doctored to remain, black; like all his other features, they were delicately and clearly outlined.

Reason enough, all this, for him to have been given the nickname 'Dainty'. But there were others. His suits, for example. And his shoes. He had three suits woven in hopsack, in improbable colours – one in green, one in purple, and one in a kind of mauve. Each of these suits had a matching pair of suede shoes. They would have made him an extravagant figure almost anywhere, let alone in a drab, dusty mining town like Kimberley. He was a glory to see as he came to work each morning, along the sandy driveway of the school, between two lines of whitewashed boulders, past rugby fields of sand, tennis courts of sand, iron bike sheds thrust down on the sand, and the stretches of veld in its pristine state – all rock outcrop, thorn trees, and tussocks of dry grass – of which the rest of the school grounds consisted. Ahead of him were the tall, white, Cape Dutch gables and the orange roof-tiles of the school buildings, ranged imposingly around two gravelled quadrangles. As he walked, swaying his shoulders, carrying himself upright, he held one hand to the pipe in his mouth; the other gripped his briefcase or simply swung free, more or less at a right angle to his wrist. On arrival he would go briefly into the masters' common room, before emerging from it in order to talk to the senior boys who were gathering in their quadrangle, while they waited to file into the hall for morning assembly. On the whole he preferred their company to that of his fellow teachers.

He produced the annual school play and sometimes acted in it; he always painted the scenery for it; he also painted landscapes in oils which he exhibited in town. In speaking he used an archaic, affected slang ('bags' for trousers, and 'Mr Doodah' for someone whose name he had forgotten); his accent owed nothing to Birmingham, in England, where he had been born and had gone to university, and everything to his notion of how a product of a 'good' school and a graduate of Oxford or Cambridge should speak. Yet for all his extravagance he had no difficulty in maintaining discipline in his classes. He evidently enjoyed being in the boys' company and they responded to this; he was a good mimic but did not use his skill to humiliate vulnerable members of the class; he could always rely on the approval of the little court of actors and athletes he gathered around him. We all knew that he was homosexual – the nickname given to him shows how well we knew it – and yet those of us who were not among his favourites never quite believed it; I mean, we could not believe that he actually *did* anything with anyone. We were wrong about this, as I was to learn much later, after I had left the school; but I don't think it would have made much difference to our attitude even if we had known the truth. His name was his character, and his character was an institution: a glamorous and unusual one, as far as we were concerned. Everything contributed to the effect he made; not least the fact that he came from distant, metropolitan England, the country to which English-speaking South Africans used to turn automatically for support in the face of virtually everything around them: Afrikaners, blacks, Cape Coloureds, Indians, veld, heat, sand.

This was the man who read the passage from *Eothen* in which the word 'chemise' appeared. Actually it took the form, in the book, of 'chemisette'. In coy, facetious fashion, Kinglake listed various garments worn by Middle Eastern ladies of the higher classes; the list ended with the phrase 'sweet chemisette'. At that point Dainty paused from his reading, looked up, and explained to us that 'chemisette' was of course the diminutive of 'chemise'. We all knew what a chemise was, didn't we?

Well, didn't we?

At some point in the silence that followed, I became aware that several of the boys were looking at me. I was the word-expert among them. Dainty was looking at me too, one eyebrow raised interrogatively. To my embarrassment I had to admit that the word was new to me.

So? Could I guess what it meant?

Obviously it was something that women wore. What, I did not know.

Dainty went to the blackboard and wrote up the word, in his clear, schoolmasterly hand. Then he returned to his chair, which, as always, he had moved away from his desk and put down directly in front of us and on a level with us. He settled himself comfortably in it, legs apart and stretched out before him. His eyes found mine again. He took a fold of the fine cloth of his shirt between thumb and forefinger, at the level of his nipple, and pulled it away from his body, towards us. For a moment he rubbed the cloth backwards and forwards between his fingers. The room was so quiet we could all hear the sound: furtive, dry, tiny, no sooner picked up than lost.

But as to what a chemise actually was – no, that we were not to be told. All he did was to repeat the word slowly, so slowly that we could hear it gathering, as it were, in the roof of his mouth, before being pushed out between his closing and opening lips, with the final hiss following at leisure behind. As he said the word it seemed to me that I could almost hear the sound of underwear clinging to and caressing the bodies it covered; it was as if I could feel under my fingers the sheen and softness of the garments, their slitheriness, their readiness softly to crumple. The secrets Dainty was perversely both withholding and disclosing in the affected, lingering stress of his voice, in the gesture with which he still held his shirt away from his body, in the lascivious distaste and pleasure of his smile, were secrets to me no longer. They were all in the word: in the word only! If you knew a word like that you could use it; if you used it, its power became yours. Words were not signs or posters pointing to meanings outside themselves; they *were* their meanings. In their spelling, in their sound, in the place they assumed among others, in the very movements of your tongue and lips and throat as you said them and the movement of your mind as you thought them, you entered their life and they entered yours.

I could not have said any of this at the time – words for it were precisely what I lacked – but it was what I felt. In his own fashion, and for his own reasons, Dainty must have been swayed by feelings resembling my own, since he was plainly reluctant either to abandon the word and go on with the next paragraph of the book, or to relieve me of his intense, half-teasing gaze. He was now no longer holding the breast of his shirt away from him; his hands were flat on his thighs. Did any of us, he asked, know the plural of the word?

Several boys cried out (in effect), 'Shemeezes!'

I knew there had to be a catch in the question or Dainty would not have asked it; and he knew that I knew. All I could think of, as I lifted my eyes from his in order to stare at the word he had written on the blackboard, was that if you took off the last 'e' and put a 't' there, the letters would spell out 'chemist' instead. How different it would sound then! How different it would be! How utterly unlike a garment that women wore next to their skins!

'The plural of "chemise",' Dainty told us, 'is "chemises".'

Of course we could hear no difference in the pronunciation of the two forms of the word. Finally someone asked if it was one of those words that stayed the same in the plural. Like 'sheep'.

'No, not like "sheep",' Dainty said scornfully. He got up, went to the blackboard, and added an 's' to what he had written there. Once again he returned to his seat. He was now openly smiling.

We were all mystified. Tuition in French was not available in the school. French plurals were unknown. Everyone had to study Afrikaans; if you wanted to do an extra language, Latin was available; nothing else. So Dainty had to explain this curious plural to us, which he did with many other examples from the French, and with many insults familiar to us from previous lessons: what an uncouth lot we were, barbarians, colonials, ignoramuses. These epithets were uttered quite cosily, in the tone in which they were usually uttered. More than ever his explanation made the word which had provoked it seem both exotic and intimate; the one as much as the other, the one because the other.

At long last the subject was exhausted. Dainty had to go back to the book. I felt released from the mocking challenge he had been putting to me. No sooner had he started reading than the bell rang. The lesson was over. School was over for the afternoon.

Amazed at what had happened in the course of the lesson, I went outside. Nothing had happened: a word had been said several times and written once on the blackboard, some glances had been exchanged between a teacher and myself, a gesture had been made, a few questions asked and answered. Yet I felt a kind of exaltation as I came out of the school buildings. Everything I saw seemed to be more wholly itself, more fully charged with itself, than it had ever been before. The sky overhead was cloudless, flawless, yet it already had a ruddy, metallic gleam or sheen to it, a forewarning of the colours that would flare across it a few hours hence. Across the pallid intensities of the school grounds there moved the upright figures of boys going home; some on foot, some cycling. There was a gang of convicts – Africans, in red blouses, their spindly legs sticking out of baggy, cream-coloured shorts – who were clearing rocks and grass near the gate. Their feet were bare. They were guarded by another black, in uniform, with a flat-bladed spear in his hand. No one thought to be ashamed that these scarecrow figures of dejection and deprivation, some of them no older than the oldest boys in the school, should be employed to level our rugby fields or to whitewash the stones along the driveway; no one saw anything incongruous in the contrast between our school outfits of blazer and tie and their blouses and pants. As I rode by them on my bicycle, a couple of them looked up from their work, as they were always ready to do. Our eyes met; their gaze told me nothing but that I had passed across it, as close to them and as remote from them as a figure in a dream.

Then I was out in the street. Up Memorial Road, on their bicycles, in their green summer tunics, their legs bare but for the white socks at their ankles, came the first of the girls from what was called our 'sister school', the Kimberley Girls High School. None of the girls who passed were known to me. The most I had ever done with such girls, conversing aside, was to kiss a few of them, to touch or fondle even fewer. But I no longer felt disadvantaged and ignorant at the sight of them. I had an advantage over them I had never previously had. It had been given to me in the course of that lesson and I would never lose it. I knew that under their tunics, somewhere against their bodies, they all wore chemises! I could spell the word in its singular and plural forms, and pronounce it in both. The power it contained was now mine. It was just one word among an infinite number of others to which I could gain access and through which I could reveal to everyone – to those girls, to the boys straggling out of school behind me, even perhaps to the convicts – what they would not otherwise have known about themselves.

In a sense I am still living with the consequences of that moment of elation, and its strange mingling of space and colour, conviction and movement, sexual urgency and something I can only call slyness. This tale itself is, obviously enough, one of those consequences. Yet it seems right to end it by describing what followed immediately afterwards. The relationship between Dainty and me took a different turn after that lesson: perhaps as a result of it, perhaps for some other reason of which I was unaware. He did not invite me to join his court or clique; I was not asked to tea at his house or to take part in any of his theatrical productions. However, from time to time subsequently, without ever offering me a word of either written or spoken explanation, he used to leave little presents in my desk. I would find them there in the morning when I unpacked my bag, or after the lunchtime break. It might be a copy of *The New Statesman*, from London, to which he was a subscriber, or an anthology of poems for schools which he no longer used; once, I remember, it was a coloured picture postcard of John Barrymore as Hamlet. The moment I saw the first of these gifts I knew from whom it must have come. To be their recipient was as embarrassing as it was flattering; but I was touched by them, too, and somehow all the more touched by their modesty, which I have no doubt was carefully judged. When I thanked him he simply smiled and waved me away. I wanted also to say something to him about what he had done for me in revealing and releasing the life that could be found in a single word. But of course I never did. I did not dare to.

LONG
WEEKEND

The cities of Kimberley and Bloemfontein lie about a hundred miles apart. Considering that there is little between them but parched, pale veld, wire fences, and tin-roofed farmhouses, one would think there would be a fair amount of coming and going between the two places. Perhaps this does take place nowadays. When I lived in Kimberley, however, the two towns stood aloof from one another. There were many reasons for this. Chief among them was the fact that the whites of Kimberley were at that time almost wholly English-speaking; Bloemfontein, the former capital of the Boer Republic of the Orange Free State, was 'Dutch', or Afrikaans-speaking; the result was a gulf that nothing could bridge. Moreover, Kimberley people nursed a secret resentment against Bloemfontein simply because it was bigger and better endowed: it was a provincial capital, which Kimberley was not; it was the seat of the country's Supreme Court; it housed a college of the University of South Africa. Not that the effect of these advantages should be exaggerated. If you did go to Bloemfontein, what did you find there? A few more cinemas than in Kimberley, two or three more department stores, a zoo, a few 'historic' buildings of granite, dating from the days of the Boer Republic, the same heat, the same flat countryside all around (even more denuded of trees than it was around Kimberley); nothing to make you feel that the journey had been worthwhile. Better by far, if you were vacation-bound, to turn your car northwards to the big-city excitements of Johannesburg, or southwards to the spectacularly heaped and fractured coastlines of the Cape.

At some time during my adolescence, however, the towns' two small Jewish communities, each of which consisted of about a hundred and twenty families, decided that they should do more for one another and with one another than they had done in the past. As far as the young people were concerned, this meant that a group from each town visited the other for a long weekend, turn and turn about, every six months or so. The arrangement came to an abrupt end after a couple of years, in the circumstances I shall describe below; but while it lasted it made a welcome change for anyone, like myself, who belonged to either group. Boys and girls were put up in each other's houses; a programme of events of various kinds, from lectures to rugby matches, was arranged; in the free time between these events there was ample opportunity for driving about in motor cars or walking about the streets late at night, playing ping-pong, gossiping, smoking, public flirting, private pairing-off, and some drinking. Almost all of it was as innocent as it was intense; most childish perhaps in its most nervously grown-up moments; the kind of thing that similar groups of prosperous, middle-class, secularised young Jews in Europe would no doubt have been doing during those very years, if the Nazis had not been rounding them up and murdering them.

In the course of one such weekend a picnic was arranged at a place called Riverton, on the Vaal River, about fifteen miles outside Kimberley. A bus was hired to take out those who could not get a lift in a private car. There must have been about forty in the party altogether; the oldest perhaps nineteen years of age, the youngest thirteen; about half were visitors from Bloemfontein. On the way out people talked to one another and showed off as they usually did; from time to time, though, they also put their heads solemnly together and exchanged whispers and glances and meaningful nods. They were talking about a scene that had taken place after a dance the previous night. Two of the Kimberley boys, one named Brian, the other John, had got drunk at the dance and had then gone to the house of one of the girls in the group. There they had behaved so badly that the girl had finally told them to clear out. The scene

that followed was noisier and nastier still. The girl's parents became involved; the two youngsters were manhandled out of the
house; alternately yelling insults and weeping, Brian stood in the
lamplit street, which a few minutes before had been as tranquil as
only a small-town, residential street, late at night, can be. He
knew why he'd been treated like that, he cried; people liked to
push him around; they thought of him as a cripple; they despised
him because of it; but he'd show them all one day; and so forth.

The scene – with all its varying proportions of melodrama,
misery, excitement, and pleasure for everybody involved – ended
as such scenes usually do. After much expostulation and explanation, more tears and expressions of defiance and apology, everyone dispersed into the darkness. Now it was all over, or would
have been all over, but for two things. The first was that people
had begun to suspect that John had what would nowadays be
called a 'serious drink problem'. He was a silly, giggling schoolboy,
nothing more, fully sixteen years old, with a pair of jaunty shoulders
and a face ravaged by acne. That he might also be on the way to
becoming a 'real' drunk, a grown-up drunk, a helpless drunk, was
no longer impossible to conceive, as it had been a few months
before, but merely implausible; too grandiose, somehow. As
things turned out, this wonder or suspicion among some of those
who knew him was not at all a piece of adolescent sensationalism:
much of the next fifteen years or more of John's life was to be spent
either in a state of drunkenness or in various institutions for the
treatment of alcoholism. Then his irreparably damaged liver
finally gave up the struggle.

As for Brian – bespectacled, bony-browed Brian, whose left
hand clutched his hip as he walked and whose frail chest was somehow a little closer to his chin than one would ordinarily expect
chest and chin to be; Brian with his prominent, flattish nose and
lizard-like smile, his curiously harsh voice and grunting laugh,
which always seemed to be shaken out of him in small bursts of
sound, as if he were reluctant to let it go; brown-haired, faintly
freckled, sardonic Brian, who was older than almost everyone else

in the group, and who looked even older than his years, partly because of his stooped walk and partly because of an habitual weariness and wariness around the eyes – Brian was quite a different case. His friends cared about him far more than they ever would about poor John. Whether or not John drank too much, or why he drank too much, were subjects for gossip rather than real concern. There are always people like John, whose claims to attention are easily put by, without their acquaintances even realising that that is what they are doing to them. There are also people of whom the exact opposite is true. Though they may not seem to wish it, or even to know it, their presence penetrates and changes and appears to enlarge the possibilities open to the company they keep. Brian was one of these. He was not a 'leader', but something more interesting. He roused your curiosity. You wanted him to share his experiences with you. Your expectations became keener when you saw his curiosity stir. It was a knack or gift he had; like all gifts it was irreducible, beyond explanation, as much part of him as the texture of his skin or the posture of his body or, for that matter, his habit of wearing his shirt-sleeves only half rolled up, to just below the elbows.

Why should the movement of his body in his shirt, even the buttons on one particular blue, coarse-woven shirt, still be vivid in my memory after so many years? The question is impossible to answer. The detail is simply lodged in my mind, among many others. For a long time he and my older brother had been close friends, which meant that though I saw him often I never had a direct relationship with him; they were the ones who decided whether or not I would be allowed to join their games or conversations. Then they drifted apart and I saw much less of him. But between us there remained something of the closeness and distance of the earlier relationship. I was more than just another junior to him, and he showed it in the way he looked at me and talked to me. Or did not talk to me. He and I sometimes used to walk part of the way home together, after school: strangely enough, given his vivacity at other times, what I remember best about those walks was their unembarrassed, almost intimate silence. It was as if he did not mind my seeing just how fatigued an ordinary day at school could make him feel. His face would be set, his walk more laboured than usual, his forehead somehow more prominent.

My other memories of him, though, are quite different in kind. Once, when he and my brother were having an 'insults match' – trading the worst things they could say about each other – Brian fell silent and then brought out his *coup de grâce*: 'Well, whatever I am, you're what comes out of my arse.' It was the end of the match. My brother conceded defeat by collapsing helplessly into laughter. Brian merely smiled like a lizard. Thereafter he had merely to say warningly, 'Remember where you come from,' to recall and even to reproduce his triumph. On another occasion, when my brother was jeering at one of the boys in his class for being a 'swot' and a 'creeper', Brian, who must have been about thirteen at the time, said off-handedly, 'You talk like a fool. He knows what the school's there for. It's to teach him things.' It wasn't the wisdom of the remark that was impressive, but its self-assurance, and its disinterestedness too, for though Brian was clever enough at his books he was no 'swot' or 'creeper' himself. (The boy they were talking about, incidentally, was eventually to settle in Canada and become a millionaire in the electronics industry.) On yet another occasion I remember Brian patiently teaching a barefoot African child whom we had come across in some dusty street, and who had no English at all, to repeat after him, 'Workers of the world unite. You have nothing to lose but your chains.' Timid, bewildered, suspicious, yet pleased at having been noticed and eager to enter this incomprehensible game, the boy obliged. After about half-a-dozen attempts he had it by heart. Brian told him to remember the words – they were very strong *muti* (magic) – and dismissed him. The child ran off, his lips still moving over the phrases.

He was different. There was nobody else at school or outside it about whom one could have told such stories. There was no one else whose words, whose gaze, whose demeanour, even when he was fooling about, were marked by such a curiously watchful restraint or detachment; a distancing of himself from what he was doing, which made the activity seem all the more intense to the people around him. This capacity or quality, I have no doubt, sprang in part from the fact that he had suffered from a severe and prolonged illness as a child. He had had polio at the age of about eight, and had almost died of it. For weeks, to make matters worse, the disease had been misdiagnosed as tick fever. Then there had followed many months in bed, endless physiotherapy sessions, a trip to the United States just before the outbreak of the war, where his distraught (and wealthy) parents had taken him in search of some kind of miracle cure. In the end the degree of disability with which the disease had left him was not as severe, apparently, as had at first been feared: he suffered from a permanent weakness of the spine which showed itself in the way he walked (his hand supporting his hip) and the posture of his body. He had lost a year or more of school and had fallen out of my brother's class into the one immediately above my own. He had difficulty in walking for long distances or in standing for long periods; he was also barred from all organised sports. On the other hand, because of the physiotherapy and hydrotherapy courses he had been through, he was supposed to be a powerful swimmer.

I had never heard him talk of his illness or of its after-effects, not even to my brother when they had been close to one another; nor had anyone ever said to me that Brian had spoken to him (or her) about it. Now he himself, after the dance, had ruptured the privacy he had jealously preserved over many years. He had stood in the middle of a street, outside the house of a girl he was especially fond of, and had lacerated himself and everyone around him by yelling out unsayable things about his own body and about what he thought to be the attitude of others towards it. It was true that he had been drunk; lately he had been getting drunk almost as often as John; John was said to be a 'bad influence' on him. (Though there was something absurd about the idea of John's influencing anyone, Brian particularly.) But did his drunkenness cast doubt on what he had revealed about his own feelings, or was it some kind of warranty of the truth of that revelation? And how was one to talk to him now, and what would he say? If it came to that, would he even turn up for the picnic?

He did. So did John. My memory (which may be at fault here, because of what happened later) is that he and John travelled on the bus and sat together on it. What I am sure of is that I did not speak to either until we had reached our destination. The journey was not a long one. There was nothing to tell you, as you approached Riverton across the bare veld, that a pleasure resort of any kind lay ahead of you. At a cattle-crossing stood a small kiosk where an admission ticket had to be purchased; nearby was a one-room country store, closed for the weekend, with the inevitable enamel advertisement signs for Mazawattee Tea and Zam-Buk Ointment adorning its rickety frontage; scattered behind it at random on the stony, shadeless earth, were the equally inevitable African huts of mud and beaten tin. Once you were waved over the grid, you followed the road as it wound among some hollows of stone and scrub, where entire orchestras or factories of cicadas were at work, sawing their legs off.

Then Riverton appeared. First, the pumping-station for the Kimberley waterworks. Then a tea room. Small rondavels, or holiday huts, with circular white walls and pointed, thatched roofs. Some stone barbecue pits among thick-trunked, thin-leaved willow trees. A children's playground. More willows and thorn bushes, with parked cars and tents lurking among them. Gum trees. No grass: instead, the earth, which had been flooded earlier in the summer, had dried out into crisp, polygonal flakes, each one turned up at its edges, which crackled underfoot and turned instantly to dust. Dotted among the trees, facing away from the water, painted signs read CAUTION: THIS RIVER IS DEEP, WIDE, AND DANGEROUS. Only when you had gone past the signs did you come to the water, which had previously shown itself by way of intermittent flashes piercing the dangling leaves of the willows.

At least two or three hundred yards wide at that point, the river ran strongly, all its moving width exposed to the sun. On the far bank the view closed on a tangled growth of thorn. As you approached it, the water looked green, with fugitive golden glints cupped moment by moment in its myriads of shifting hollows; the sunlight recoiled from this complicated surface, which seemed to be travelling too fast to be penetrated. When you stood on the bank, directly over the water, it was neither green nor gold, but a pale brown or khaki, full of swimming particles which thickened and darkened just about two feet below. Look up again, and your dazzled eye saw the whole expanse of the river as black, like a great metalled roadway, with the bank on the other side indistinguishable from the suddenly livid sky. Then you would blink and know where you were again.

The bus and the few accompanying cars disgorged their passengers, who immediately scattered in various directions: some to the tea room, some to swim, some to look for the lavatories, some to prostrate themselves on rugs and groundsheets, some to gather wood for the barbecues they were planning. I wanted to hire a boat and had a few words about this with Brian. He wasn't interested; he was going to swim, he said; with a certain amount of bravado, and a faint grin, he added that a swim was just the thing for his hangover. I was with the girl at whose house the row had taken place the previous night. Short-haired, brown-eyed, smooth-skinned, the owner of a voice so high in pitch people were sure she put it on for effect, she was no spoil-sport – anything but – and we all knew it. There did not seem to be any special constraint between her and Brian. They must have already made up in some way, perhaps on the telephone. In the end, he and John and a couple of others went one way; the girl and I and two companions went to the place where the boats for hire were moored. When we got there we found that none was available for the moment. So we had a swim instead. The current felt as strong as it had looked, and the water was quite cold. But the one really disagreeable part of the swim was the thick mud underfoot as you waded out to a depth where swimming was possible. Once you had taken half-a-dozen strokes the bottom disappeared. Only after the swim did we manage to get hold of a rowing boat, in which we set out for the middle of the river.

There were many other boats on the water and many people swimming about, most near the bank, others farther out. The boat had been hired for an hour, but we did not keep it nearly that long: the sun was too hot, out in the open, and anyway we decided we were getting hungry. So we returned the boat to its mooring-place and started walking back, alongside the river, to the place where the bus and cars were parked, in order to pick up our modest hampers. We hadn't gone far when we suddenly heard cries – the first we had heard – from a boat which was just a few yards away. It was approaching directly towards us, at right angles to the bank. It hit the bank prow first. Several boys we knew leapt up from it with an agitated clatter and rumble of oars and rowlocks. Behind them, a person reared up within the boat; then we saw that he had risen in that fashion because the others were hauling and pushing him upright; then we saw that it was Brian. Amid shouts and gasps he was stumblingly carried on to the bank and laid down on it.

He died there, in front of us. His face was turned to one side. It was blue in colour. It had an intent, inward expression, as if he were listening to a voice within him which might have been lost if he had been distracted by the efforts of the people working over him, or by the crowd that gathered at a little distance to gaze at the scene. I had witnessed only one death before; also that of a boy; someone from school whom I knew slightly; I had come on him, around a corner, seconds only after he had been knocked off his bicycle by a speeding army truck, and then carried by it for many yards before being thrown off it. He had been so badly smashed up that it was those parts of his body which were still undamaged, ordinary, apparently unaware of what had happened to the rest of him, that looked uncanny or bizarre. Brian was not like that. Only his colour and the intentness of his expression seemed to tell one that there was no more to be done in this case than there had been in the other.

What could be done, was done. People worked over him for I don't know how long; hours it seemed. Much of the work was carried out by one of the visitors from Bloemfontein: himself, ironically enough, a champion swimmer, the holder of a junior South African title. He was the one who had held Brian up in the water after he had collapsed. John and Brian had been swimming together; it was John's voice, in fact, not Brian's, which had made the visitor realise that something serious was amiss. An ambulance and a doctor were summoned from Kimberley; someone, I don't know who, also telephoned Brian's parents. While they waited for the professionals to arrive, the amateur helpers continued to toil away at their task. Those, like myself, who had no expertise in first-aid, wandered away and came back – once because there was a cry of, 'He's coming round, he's coming round!' which turned out to have nothing in it. But I remember that when I heard the cry I thought, '*Of course* he's coming round!' as though Brian and I had all along had a silent understanding, one quite private to ourselves, that he would do so. I remember also sitting with three or four others on the thick root of a willow tree that grew out of the ground. It was near the river, which was now sullenly empty of boats and bathers. During that time all of us, I think, got to know how grey the dust was, how grooved was the root, how hot the sunlight, how stricken in appearance faces could become, how little breath there seemed to be in anyone's chest, how dark it was when you put your hands over your face.

The ambulance men and the doctor eventually arrived. They too set to work. But they were able to do no more than the others. Brian's parents arrived just after the effort had been abandoned, and the body had been carried into the ambulance. The doors of the ambulance had just been closed when their car came to a halt. The doctor went to them. Brian's mother cried, 'My boy, my baby boy!' and his father clapped his hands loudly together in front of his chest.

Then, and only then, it seemed, was it over: truly irrevocable. We got in the vehicles which had brought us to the river and returned to Kimberley. None of the visitors from Bloemfontein stayed for the funeral, which had to be postponed until after the inquest. (Its finding was that Brian had not drowned but had died of coronary failure.) No one could bring himself to suggest, the following year, that there should be another exchange between the young people of the Jewish communities in the two towns; indeed, no further visits of that kind took place while I still lived in Kimberley.

Brian was the forerunner. With his high spirits and his detachment, his frailty and his strength of will, his laughter and the element of grimness in him, he had always seemed the most grown-up among us. His death made it seem as if he would have that advantage over us forever. But today, forty years after the events I have described, several others who went on that outing to Riverton lie alongside him in the Kimberley Jewish cemetery. One by one we are at last catching up with him.

PART
TWO

TIME
OF ARRIVAL

It was just after midday that the boat docked at Dover. We went through the Customs shed and on to the pallid grey platform of the railway station. With all the anxieties of arrival upon me, in England for the first time, a few days after my twenty-first birthday, I nevertheless felt at peace. One could not help feeling at peace, the station was so quiet, the officials were so homely in appearance, the voices of the passengers were raised in such a clear, almost bird-like way. I bought *The Times* and the *New Statesman*, and felt with gratification, after years of handling only the overseas editions, the thickness of the paper between my fingers; with the same gratification I saw the dateline on the papers to be the actual date, not that of two or three weeks before. So I was in England, truly in England at last. I had not known how much I had wanted to be in England until then; until, on that platform, an anxiety came to rest, and something else within me – an ambition perhaps, or a hope – began to stir.

I remember vividly those casual yet oddly decisive moments on Dover station, and the very different moment of arrival at Victoria, but nothing of the journey between. Victoria seemed huge to me, echoing, dark; black-clothed people scurried bewilderingly under the vault, in all directions. Fortunately, I was travelling with my brother, who had been in London before, and knew his way about the city a little. As it was still early in the afternoon we decided we would not bother for the moment about finding accommodation, but would simply leave our luggage in the station cloakroom and go out for a look around.

The pavements outside were a little paler than the overcast sky; the cobbled space in front of the station seemed overcrowded with lumbering red buses. We did not go far on that first exploration; we merely caught one of the buses to Hyde Park Corner, crossed into the park, and walked up towards Marble Arch. Already, on that walk, I was struck by what was for me to be one of London's most surprising features: its spaciousness, the size of its streets, squares and public places. (The size of the city itself was another matter, and quite distinct from what I am speaking of here: in a way, the area the city as a whole covered did not come as such a surprise to me, partly because I could not, and still cannot, grasp it: it is beyond reckoning, beyond the widest span of one's imagination.) I suppose I had heard so much about the 'tight little island', about England being 'cramped', 'crowded', and 'pinched' – and had also heard so much about the 'wide open spaces' of South Africa, about the 'vastness' of the veld – that somehow in my mind there was an expectation that everything in England would really be small, reduced in scale, somehow toylike. And it was true that many of the individual buildings were small, and did seem to have been rammed against one another, in a frozen jostle for space. Nevertheless, again and again, on other walks, I was to be surprised by such random things as the sheer mass of the piers and arches of bridges; the width of the steps leading up to monuments; the striving, swaying height of the trees in the parks, and the breadth of the expanses of grass around them; the acres upon acres of the city given over to railways gleaming in parallel lines; the stretches of terraced houses which seemed to wear their encrusted ornamentation like a frown, and which stood in endless repetition down wide, windblown streets.

On that first walk it was Hyde Park itself which was imposing, and the lumps of statuary just inside and outside the park, and the glimpses of streets and buildings beyond. It was mid-afternoon, in late March, and bitterly cold; there seemed to be nothing spring-like in the air, though I was surprised to see how green was the grass in the park. From nowhere, it seemed, a gust of rain was suddenly dashed into our faces as we walked; it did not seem at all to have come from the sky. The gust ceased as abruptly as it had begun. But the sun did not come out; it looked as though the sun never had come out, and never would. Through the streets, between the trees, over the grass, the light *moved*. That is the only way I can describe the thickness of the light; the swiftness with which it changed; the slightness of the individual changes; the way it could change at a distance and yet remain unchanged nearby. It was as if between ourselves and the source of light there had been put an infinite number of filters, which were constantly being removed and replaced, nearer and farther in a perpetual alternation.

Within this shifting light, colours had a strange intensity; they seemed to well up continuously within each object, instead of being a static, hard, settled dye or tone. Because of this suffusion or seepage of colour, one almost expected the objects themselves to be vague in outline, to run together, so their precision and firmness of line came invariably as a surprise. This was true even of the faces of people, which were either vague or suddenly vivid, featureless or disconcertingly quick in expression. Even on that first walk I saw how fine, how subtle, how eccentric the faces of the English were. Each face seemed to carry within it the shadows, the suggestions, of innumerable others which had neither come to the surface nor been entirely lost.

Unexpectedly, it began to grow dark, really dark, though it was not yet five o'clock. So we had to think of finding an hotel, and went back from Marble Arch to Victoria to collect our luggage. My brother knew that there were many cheap hotels in Bloomsbury. We told a taxi-driver simply to take us there; he drove to Tavistock Square, and we stopped him at the first hotel we saw. It was a narrow converted house. Everything inside it was narrow too: the entrance-hall, the manager's cubicle, the manager's face, the staircase, the room into which we were eventually shown. The room smelled heavily of damp; it had a single large window, overlooking a fire-escape and a brick wall; right against the sky, above everything else, a battery of chimney-pots stood poised. An Irish maid came in to make up the beds; an elderly woman, with eyes that seemed to move about too much, under a tired, deeply lined brow. She was silent throughout, until my brother went out of the room; then she came up to me, took my arm with her hand in a fierce grip, brought her face close to mine and said passionately, 'You're lucky there's the two of you. It gets too queer when you're alone!' A moment later she was gone.

Quite by chance I had been reading on my way to England a miscellany which contained, among other things, a collection of letters written by Virginia Woolf to Logan Pearsall Smith. The letters had been addressed, I remembered, from Tavistock Square. The first thing I did was to get the book from my suitcase and look up the number of the house she had lived in. When we came out of the hotel we walked around the square, looking for the house among the black, flat-fronted dwellings which remained on two sides of it. The house itself, however, no longer existed. In its place was a bomb-site. We leaned over a low brick wall, looking into the hole in the ground where the house should have been. Down below were stumps of walls, some of them overgrown, others showing bits of coloured plaster and tile. Great wooden beams rose out of the hole to buttress the building from which the one on this site had been severed.

I must have spent hours, during my first few weeks in London, looking into such bomb-sites, wondering about them, searching in myself for a response to them which seemed adequate, and never finding it. Many of the ruins were dramatic, even melodramatic, to look at, with bare walls as flat as shadows, and the sky showing through gaps which had once been doors and windows; others were merely quiet, wasted, charred spaces, where only a few ledges and bits of brick revealed the basements of what had once been houses, churches, office-blocks, blocks of flats. How could such weights of masonry have been brought down by flame and explosion into heaps of rubble? How had the rubble been carted away, leaving the streets trim, though gaping? In the end one had to look at the ruins as one looked at everything else: as part of the spectacle of London, as another sign of the things that people had done over the hundreds of years they had been in London, just another evidence of their having lived and died in the place.

Anyway, the house Virginia Woolf had written those letters from was no longer there, and I was disappointed to see this. But the rest of the square was presumably much as it had been when she had been alive and had written her letters to Logan Pearsall Smith. He and she had exchanged elaborate, self-conscious mock-insults about 'Chelsea', which he was supposed to represent, and 'Bloomsbury', which of course had been hers. Part of what they had meant by Bloomsbury I saw to be these trees and houses, the glimpses above them of some of the buildings of London University, the traffic in Southampton Row. Was there nothing else? Within the disappointment that the house should have been scooped out of the square another began to grow. So this was it. I had seen it. True, I had not seen, and thought it unlikely I would ever see, any of the people who had made up the Bloomsbury society; but the physical Bloomsbury was about me. The disappointment was not with its appearance, which was black enough, and severe enough, and imposing enough; it arose from the very fact of my having seen it. The half-conscious, always-unfinished guesswork which had been so inextricably an aspect of my reading, throughout my childhood and adolescence in South Africa, the dreamlike otherness or remoteness in the books I had read, which I had valued more than I had supposed, were being taken from me, bit by bit. Here was one bit of it gone. I would never again be able to visit a Bloomsbury of my own imagination – a district vaguer and therefore more glamorous than the reality; one less hard and angular and self-defining. I would not have exchanged my glimpse of the Bloomsbury of brick and tar, of tree-trunk and iron railing, for anything I might have been able to imagine; but still, there was a loss.

Another loss I knew was my own imagination of myself in

Bloomsbury, or anywhere else in London. Coming to London had not – not yet, at any rate – changed me, transformed me, made a new man of me. Bloomsbury was what it had been before I had seen it. So was I.

Breakfasts in the hotel were gloomy meals, taken in a small dining room where everybody spoke in subdued tones, but for one man in a checked suit who rustled his *Daily Telegraph* loudly and demanded almost every morning, in a voice that carried across the room, that they give the 'cat' to the 'hooligans' whose doings he read about in the papers. He was strong on 'niggers' too. He was like a caricature of the hanging, flogging Englishman of the most benighted kind: seething with grievances and rages which reddened his round face, thickened his voice, and made his small blond moustache bristle. Did he have any suspicion of the social changes to come over the next few decades? I think not. He was my first living exemplar of the English flair for self-imitation; the zeal, the whole-heartedness with which many Englishmen conform to certain ideal types of such familiarity, not to say staleness, that the outsider positively expects some 'real' man buried within the type to give him a secret wink of irony, a little gesture or nod of complicity. But the outsider waits in vain. The man (or woman) is absorbed completely in his role. Don or dustman, *New Statesman* intellectual or flogging Tory, debutante or char: it is impossible to say which came first, the type or the individual. So it was with this man; and so too, in a different way, it was with the other guests in the hotel, who appeared to be either students or a few elderly ladies who lived there permanently. (There were no foreigners among them, apart from ourselves.) None of the other guests ever argued with or even commented upon the remarks of the hanger and flogger. Instead, in a curious, dismal, English fashion they managed wordlessly to dissociate themselves from him without putting forward any views of their own. Indeed, still wordlessly, they even managed to suggest that it wasn't so much the man's views they disapproved of, as the vehemence with which he put them forward. The hotel, incidentally, unlike others in the neighborhood, did not have a single African or Indian guest.

Breakfast was the only meal we took in the hotel: most of the time, by day and in the evenings too, we were out sightseeing. We went to Westminster Abbey; we wandered about the Strand, and St Paul's and the City: we stood in Piccadilly and Parliament Square; we went to Downing Street and across St James's Park and into Mayfair. As we went about I hardly knew whether I was actually seeing the streets and buildings in front of me or merely confirming that they were there, as the pictures and books had told me they would be. There was deep satisfaction in this confirmation: so deep I cannot easily describe it, for it was not just the reality of the buildings that was confirmed, but also in an odd, unexpected way, my own reality too. So place ran into place into place in a progression that seemed endless in length and breadth, and was limited in other dimensions, aesthetically or historically, only by my own ignorance. At every point the progression yielded some interest; it could not help doing so, for the pleasure of confirmation did not wait upon the famous buildings or vistas, but could be roused by any ordinary street or sign, both for what it was and for being where it was. However, one great fact about London was so overwhelming that I couldn't possibly think of it as a recollection or a reminder of what I had already been told. That was the shabbiness of the city.

I think I would have found London shabby under any circumstances, during the first few weeks after my arrival, because of the sky above it: everything, I felt, must look its worst under a sky that continually trailed clouds and smoke low over the buildings, and sometimes thinned a little to reveal a sun coloured like the blood-spot in an egg. However, I had come there a few years after a war which had halted the erection of new buildings, and the repair of old ones, which had destroyed or partially destroyed thousands of others; and which had then left the country to endure a kind of siege of rationing and austerity, and their accompanying gloom. There were times when I felt that an inward dissolution would do as effectively over a wider area what the bombs had done where they had fallen, and that the blackened, gutted hulks of houses one saw everywhere were the condition towards which the whole city was slowly, inevitably sinking. The public buildings were filthy, pitted with shrapnel-scars, running with pigeon dung from every coign and eave; eminent statesmen and dead kings of stone looked out upon the world with soot-blackened faces, like coons in a grotesque carnival; but tickets and torn newspapers blew down the streets or lay in white heaps in the parks; cats bred in the bomb-sites, where people flung old shoes, tin cans, and cardboard boxes; whole suburbs of private houses were peeling, cracking, crazing, their windows unwashed, their steps unswept, their gardens untended; innumerable little cafés reeked of chips frying in stale fat; in the streets that descended the slope from Bloomsbury to King's Cross old men with beards and old women in canvas shoes wandered about, talking to themselves and warding off imaginary enemies with ragged arms. As for the rest of the people – how pale they were, what dark clothes they wore, what black homes they came from, how many of them there were swarming in the streets, queueing on the pavements, standing packed on underground escalators. You saw crowds when you left the hotel, you travelled a mile and saw crowds, another mile and more crowds, another mile the same; and around them always the same run-down, decaying, decrepit, sagging, rotten city.

One night I walked about in an area which I now suspect must have been Paddington, on my way to an address I have forgotten and so cannot return to. I remember crossing a bridge over some railway lines, and looking across the parapet to a desolation of lines, shunting and stationary trains, red and green winking lights, floodlights on tall towers, iron and brick sheds from which flames occasionally broke. It was early evening, but the sun had been gone for hours, if it had ever shown itself at all during the day, and white smoke rose in plumes from the railyard and drifted across and between the lights. It seemed as though a town, a whole country, lay beneath me, and as though the bridge I stood on spanned it all. Farther along, on the other side of the bridge, was a terrace, with a little private road running the length of the row. The houses were four or five storeys tall, and were in darkness; each had its portico in front of it, with gaunt fluted pillars holding it up. Even in the half-light one could see how dilapidated they all were; ruined, cavernous, peeling. Sheets of corrugated iron were nailed over the ground-floor windows. I knocked on the door and no one answered; by then I did not expect anyone to answer; it was obvious that I had come to the wrong place. But I did not move away immediately. Standing on that abandoned doorstep, with the hoarse sound of the railyard in my ears and the darkness of the portico over me, I felt a perverse pleasure in the fact that I did not know where I was and that the people I was looking for were no longer there. I wanted to be lonely and anonymous and to feel within myself the dissolution of all that I had been by name and background.

Yet, confusingly, this city offered me a continuity between past and present, between words and things, which I had hardly known I was seeking until it was offered to me. And past and present pointed to the future. How could I avoid dreaming of the friends I might make in London, the fame I might win there, the houses I might one day be able to enter?

I had the addresses of just two people in London, neither of whom was a friend of mine, and with whom I was unable, as it turned out, to establish any kind of friendship. I had hoped that these people would help me to find a room; in the end I found one simply by catching a train to the Finchley Road Tube Station, and then walking up the road until I came to one of those glassed-in little notice-boards, advertising rooms to let and 'light removals' and vacancies for charwomen. (I went to Finchley Road because my brother had advised me to try the Hampstead area; he had never been out to Hampstead, but had heard that it was a pleasant area to live in). Many of the notices for rooms carried discouraging messages like 'Gentiles Only' or 'British and Gentile Only' or

'No Coloureds' or even, testifying to some obscure convulsion of the English conscience, 'Regret No Coloureds'. I went to the nearest address which seemed as though it might be prepared to take me, in a street that ran directly off the Finchley Road. The house was a three-storeyed Victorian giant of a place; the house-keeper lived in the basement, a school of dancing occupied the ground floor, and the rest of it was let in single and double rooms.

The housekeeper was a woman with dyed blonde hair and a mouth painted in the shape of a Cupid's bow, even though her upper lip did not in the least have a suitable shape for one. So the bow was simply drawn on, heavily, the peak of it coming just under her nose, where a man might have worn a moustache, and the tips of it reaching into her cheeks on both sides. She looked drunken or clown-like in that paint. I never saw her without it. I never saw her drunk either. In fact, she was a quiet, artless woman who slept with one of the lodgers on the top floor, and perhaps for that reason was not given to prying into the affairs of the others in the house. And she kept the place clean. The room I was offered was small, sparsely furnished, and fitted with the inevitable, ancient gas-fire and gas-ring. But the view out of the window was a wide one; it looked over the Ministry of Food offices in the Finchley Road to the vague dark spread of South Hampstead, Kilburn, Willesden, Paddington, places whose names I did not even know.

I took my luggage into the room, and then I went to see off my brother at Waterloo Station. He was returning to South Africa. Once he had gone, I had absolutely nothing to do. I decided to go to Regent's Park. The last time I had visited it I had entered it from Baker Street; this time I got off the train at Regent's Park Station, and found myself in a place that looked nothing like the park I was slightly familiar with. Flat green plains of grass stretched away to black trees on the horizon; there was hardly a soul about, for it was mid-morning on a weekday. I began walking. The silence and emptiness around me made me feel nervous; even the pallor of

my shadow on the grass was strange. Eventually in the distance I
saw what looked like the crumbling battlements of a castle: there
seemed to be a central circular keep, and crenellated walls going
down on both sides of it. It looked ruinous, historic, ominous,
lifted up against the horizon. It was part of the zoo, I found out,
when I came closer. There were bears on the battlements. The
thought of going in to stare at the animals seemed even more
desperate than the thought of going back to my room. I continued
walking, pretty much in a circle – I had no alternative really, given
the shape of the park – and at last came out at Baker Street. From
there I did what I had been flinching from doing since I had left
my brother: I went back to my room.

The house was quiet; it was only in the afternoon that the
dancing-classes began, when the piano jangled and the floors
shook with the combined thumping of all the little girls who came
to the house carrying their dancing shoes in small cloth bags. I
looked out of the window, over the glitter of the traffic in the
Finchley Road, towards the vague blue and black spread which
was only a part of the city, and which yet stretched to the very
limit of my sight. Now that I was on my own I knew that I had
really come to London. Evidently London did not care.

Shortly after I had moved into my room, a friend in South Africa
wrote that I should look up G; I would get on well with him, my
friend promised me. This, I found out, was true enough: it would
have been true of practically anybody, for G was indiscriminately
affable and garrulous. He was a slight, stoop-shouldered man in
his middle twenties, who appeared much older than he was, because
of the prominence of his pale, bald, soft-looking scalp. G was
living with a Cockney woman, an ex-prostitute (or so G claimed),
whose previous lover was in jail, from where he wrote letters describing how he was going to 'cut up' G when he got out. G told
me all this within a few minutes of our meeting. He told me about
it not only because he was garrulous, but because he was so proud
of his girl-friend, her criminal admirer, and his own association

with them both – all of it being so far removed from the Johannes-burg, Jewish, middle-class respectability in which he had been brought up. He lived in a basement flat in Belsize Park: an ill-lit subterranean place with huge rooms, rubbish bins at its entrance, and Picasso prints on its walls. Gas-fires and electric lights seemed always to be burning in the flat, and the smell of damp was driven out at intervals only by the smell of bacon and eggs.

Maisie (or was her name Milly?) listened complacently to G's account of their situation; she was slight and fair-haired, and seemed demure enough, until she spoke. When she spoke, she swore: at the weather, at a pot she might be trying to clean, at the landlord, at G. He used to call Maisie 'my love' and 'my sweet-heart', exaggeratedly, on every possible occasion; but no endear-ment ever crossed her lips. G had a theory, I remember, that a man who thinks a thought or visualises a scene is as much an artist as the man who writes down his thought or puts the scene on canvas; and no matter what we used to begin talking about, we would sooner or later find ourselves discussing this theory. He himself was writing a novel which would, he said, demonstrate the theory: when I asked him why, in view of the nature of the theory, he bothered to write the novel, he answered with several other theories which I have altogether forgotten. But quite another answer was given by Maisie: 'Him! Write a book? That'll be the fucking day!'

Through G I met Naomi K and her husband. Like G, Naomi was South African, Jewish, and from a well-to-do home; like G again, she was in flight from all these things. She was married to a tall, bearded, pipe-smoking, more-than-faintly anti-Semitic Gentile, who used to torment her by imitating her parents' accents. ('Dey vanted Naomi to marry a nize bizhnezh boy,' he would say, charmingly.) Both Naomi and he were artists; he could afford to be more flamboyantly artistic in manner than she, since they lived off what she earned as a teacher in the nursery department of a small orthodox Jewish school. Naomi was a tiny, jumpy, black-haired woman, who was continually expressing girl-like enthusiasms

over cats, or dogs, or children, or budding trees. Derek, her husband, was enthusiastic about nothing, except perhaps puncturing
Naomi's enthusiasms, which he did with an air of great fatigue,
made all the more disdainful by the smoke that dribbled from his
lips when he spoke. She would falter and apologize; he would
dribble more smoke. On the whole it was more painful to be with
them than with G and Maisie.

These were my only friends in London at that time. I feel guilty
in writing disparagingly of them now – just as I used to feel guilty,
then, in visiting them. The guilt arose from my knowing I would
hardly have sought their company if I had had other people to
visit. But I simply knew nobody else. I used solemnly to ration
myself to seeing each couple on alternate Sundays only, I remember. At their flats, on these odd Sundays, I met a few other people
– most of them South Africans, a few of them Americans or
Australians – but I became friendly with none among them. In all,
the first months of my stay in London were as lonely as any I have
ever experienced. Even after I had got a job as a teacher at a small
private school I was as lonely after school-hours and on weekends,
as I had been before.

This loneliness I felt to be really disturbing or frightening, however, only when it was brought home to me as something else – as
a kind of inward dislodgement or displacement of my own senses.
There were two recurring, almost hallucinatory experiences which
had this effect on me. Sometimes, in the crowded streets I used to
see approaching me a man or a woman whom I had known in
Johannesburg, where I had been a student at the university. I
would feel no especial surprise at this, until, as I drew nearer, the
resemblance between the person approaching and my acquaintance
would suddenly and totally disappear. Then I would realise that
I had felt no surprise at 'seeing' X or Y or Z because I had imagined
myself to be *in* Johannesburg. The shock was always a double one:
I was shocked that I should have fallen into the fantasy, and I was
shocked on coming out of it to see around me once again the
streets of a colder, darker and infinitely bigger city. The other

experience was very similar, and usually occurred when I came out of a cinema or theatre. Being disorientated, I would look around to find the way I should go, and a few times I found myself walking perhaps half a block under the impression that in this direction lay the Melville tram terminus, or Eloff Street, or Park Station – all of which were in Johannesburg, not London. A further complication of these experiences was the fact that Johannesburg was not my home-town; merely the other big city in which I had once lived, and in which I had at times been lonely too.

I was so much the more grateful, therefore, that almost all of London, though new to me, was yet familiar in a ghostly way; and that the familiarity should have been so sustaining, even exhilarating. Everywhere I went I saw the visible, external frame or setting of much that had hitherto seemed to exist only as an abstraction within me, and that I had never truly believed could exist in any other way. Now I saw the sky under which so many imagined actions had taken place, and the streets where they had been enacted: these were the faces the protagonists had worn and these the accents in which they had spoken. It was as though some part of my imagination had been dry before, deprived of the nourishment it did not even know it needed; now, immersed in the English medium, it slowly filled itself and expanded. The medium was thicker and heavier than I could ever have anticipated; ultimately it was more burdensome too. There was so much I did not know and never would know; there was so little I could ever do, in comparison with what had been done and done and done and done a hundred thousand times, and more. Yet better that burden, I was sure, than none at all.

In the Charing Cross Road, one night, I saw the performance of an escape-artist and his assistant. By the time I joined the crowd, the artist had already been completely covered in a kind of canvas shroud, which the assistant was knotting with ropes in front and behind. The assistant was stripped to the waist, the artist was a

bundle without face or limbs, and the arena on which they per-
formed was marked out on the pavement by a long leather whip
which the audience was not supposed to cross. These trappings
were obviously intended to give the show a spicy or gamy quality.
The assistant pitched the bundle on to the ground, and then
chained it up, jocularly pushing it about, hectoring it, tugging
hard at the ropes and chains, and eventually leaving it lying on the
pavement while he went around demanding money from the
crowd. The skin of his shoulders was goose-pimpled with cold.
On the pavement the bundle breathed, but was otherwise quite
still. When the collection was over, the assistant picked up the
whip, trailed it over the ground, and suddenly lifted it as if to
strike at the creature under him. But he just cracked the whip in
the air, once, and a second time, and the bundle began writhing
and squirming, its chains rattling and tinkling against the cement
slabs, grunts and heavy breathing coming from within it. It rolled
over and over, towards the audience and back again; occasionally
it lay still before contracting and expanding in a spasm.

The man succeeded in freeing himself in the end: a wizened,
gingerish face peered morosely out of the shroud, and the audience
immediately began to disperse, as if everyone in it was ashamed of
himself. There was no applause, and the man obviously expected
none. He had escaped too many times before; and had seen too
many crowds edge guiltily away from him.

Summer came: or rather, summer slowly diffused itself. The
weather was not hot, merely warm, but the warmth was like heat
in comparison with the cold that had persisted for so long before.
I remember looking out of the window of my classroom, one
afternoon, while the boys were busy with their exercise books, and
being surprised at the sight of the sun shining directly upon the
street outside: I had never before seen it so strong and clear, in
England. Yet behind its rays there was still a blue or grey vibration
in the light, a hint of darkness. On another afternoon I took the
boys of my class on an outing to Epping Forest. The day was

overcast, but warm and windless; the brown and grey leaves of the previous autumn lay in drifts underfoot; the leaves overhead were the softest green, so soft that they seemed more an exhalation than a growth. The woods were silent, except for our own shouting and crashing through the leaves and undergrowth. When we came to an open space we played rounders, and then had lunch, the boys sharing with me the sandwiches their mothers had packed for them. After lunch it grew steadily warmer; the clouds seemed to move lower, the air to become heavier. The shouts of the boys no longer carried as they had done before, among the trees, and I brought them together and made for the road and the bus-stop, anxious lest we should be caught by the rain. But it held off until we were back among the lights and traffic and cinema posters just outside the school; then it came down briefly and boisterously; no sooner was the downpour over than the air was clear and bright again.

London in summer was very different to what it had been in the bleak, dark spring: in some ways a more relaxed city; in others, an even shabbier one, for the sun exposed much that was better concealed. The intensity of the difference was unexpected to me, for in South Africa – or at least in the part of South Africa from which I came – summer and winter look much alike. Here the days lengthened extravagantly; the trees continued to thicken and darken with foliage; people, wearing a kind of clothing they had not worn before, thronged together in the parks; whole suburbs which had previously been hidden by smoke and mist as I went on the bus to school now revealed their black and red roofs, their roads, their football fields. It seemed that in England even the calendar had visible external meanings that I had not fully understood before. And the chief of these meanings was movement; the passage of time made manifest.

II

I had got the job at the school through Naomi K who had known that the Jewish boys' school to which her kindergarten was attached had been looking for a class-master who could teach, among other things, English, History and French. French I could not teach, but I thought I could make an attempt to teach the rest. So, after Naomi had put in a word for me, I took a bus to Camden Town, changed there to another bus, and travelled for a further forty-five minutes through great tracts of London I had never seen before, to be interviewed by Mr B, the school secretary and its effective head.

Of Mr B I retained an impression, from that first interview, of little more than a pair of heavy spectacles and a black beard. Later I was to see that a smile of unexpected charm could come between the beard and the spectacles. But he did not smile the first morning I saw him – not once. He was wearing a black overcoat and a hat on the back of his head; he sat at the end of a long table, piled high with papers and exercise books, pedagogic charts and old newspapers in Yiddish and English. The room was poverty-stricken; it had a bare, battered semi-public appearance, like the committee room of an unsuccessful political party or charitable appeal. The paint on the walls was pitted; the light-shade was covered in dust. A glassed-in bookcase stood in one corner, and a desk in another. That was all its furniture, apart from the laden table and a few chairs.

Mr B laboriously wrote down in a paper-covered exercise book almost everything I said. He took down my date of birth, the name of the school I had attended, the degree I had taken in South Africa, the fact that I had no teaching experience. He did not ask me the questions I had been afraid he might ask: What was I doing in England? How long did I think I would stay? What did I want to become? These were questions to which I had no answers; or no answers which I felt I could give to Mr B. But he did ask me whether I was orthodox; or rather, he stated as a fact, in his strong East European accent, looking through his spectacles at my bare head and clean-shaven chin, 'You are not orthodox.'

'No.'

He drew a line under the words 'Bachelor of Arts, University of the Witwatersrand, Johannesburg' and wrote: 'Not orthodox'. Then he drew a line under that.

'Mrs K tells me you can't teach French?'

'No.'

He wrote that down. Then he closed the exercise book and stared at me in silence. I didn't know what he wanted me to do or say. In the silence I became aware once again of the continual murmur overhead, that I had noticed when I had first come into the building. It was a restless, shuffling, unmistakable hubbub; as characteristic as the smell of dust, schoolbooks and chalk that was in my nostrils. Under Mr B's stare, hearing that noise, my heart sank. I was too close to my own schooldays to feel anything but depression at the thought of entering a school once again, in any capacity. I would have been relieved, just then, if Mr B had told me that on considering my qualifications he had decided that I wasn't suitable for the appointment.

But he didn't say that; instead, unexpectedly, taking it for granted that the position was mine, he began explaining to me the principles on which the school was run. From eight in the morning until twelve, it was a 'Talmud Torah'. Did I know what a Talmud Torah was? The boys studied Hebrew and the Bible and the Talmud, under one group of teachers. Then, under another group, from twelve o'clock until four-thirty they studied the subjects taught in any other school. So my day would begin at twelve. I would have no duties after school hours. The salary would be six pounds ten shillings a week, and I would get a free school lunch. He would write to me confirming the arrangement. I would begin after half-term; that is, at the beginning of the next week. He stood up, and we shook hands. Only then did he say, in a calm, warning tone, 'You will remember always that this school is here to preserve Jewish orthodoxy. You will not give offence.'

'I'll try not to.'

'Good.' He nodded, gave me a last stare through his spectacles, and turned away. I went out of the room, into the bare vestibule, then into the blighted garden in front of the school, and so on to the main road, where the buses ran.

All around the school, in every direction, there were houses that must have been built at about the same time as the school itself, out of the same grey brick, with the same cream-coloured plaster frames around their windows, and the same slate roofs overhead. Few of them, however, were of the size of the school, which I imagine must once have been the home of some aspiring late-Victorian or Edwardian shopkeeper or professional man. It no longer looked the least opulent or ambitious; it fitted in unnoticeably with the entire district, which was miserably drab, featureless, shapeless, endless, with not a building or corner you could look forward to before it came, or remember when it was past.

On the way to school there were several main crossroads, with their clusters of tiled cinemas and brick tube-stations, TV and radio shops, fish-and-chip shops, branches of Woolworths and Marks and Spencer; there were many factories; there were a few iron bridges where trains passed over the road; there were perhaps a dozen garages and motor showrooms; there were one or two little parks with green grass and soot-blackened tree-trunks; for the rest, there were just those grey brick houses, smaller or larger, dirtier or cleaner, standing on the road or held back from it by tiny gardens. Travelling up and down this route, you had a glimpse of the true size of London; at any rate it was called 'London', though you had no sense of place within it. It was a mere distension of bricks and mortar, a continuation of what was already nothing but a continuation. Never, not even when the bus went into a lower gear and slowly climbed an incline, was there an end to it. You looked over roofs on to roofs, between streets into streets, from one sprawled suburb across the next.

The decrepitude of Paddington and Notting Hill, of the whole of central London was dramatic, or appeared to be so; it seemed to speak to one of all kinds of terrors and satisfactions, of as many of both as one could imagine. The shabbiness of these areas on the way to school had no voice, no accent, no meaning; at most they had a kind of pathos, which you felt when you saw the women coming out of the pinched, meagre, indistinguishable homes, carrying their shopping-bags and pushing their high-wheeled prams, or when you saw into the interiors of the little shops which the women would visit, with tins of groceries or boxes of sweets and cigarettes piled on shelves, and men in aprons leaning over counters, their hands clasped idly together and their gaze quite still but seeming to be looking at nothing.

In the middle of all this, barely a hundred yards away from one of the busiest of the road-junctions, was the —— School, devoted to the preservation of Jewish orthodoxy. Every weekday morning the boys assembled, looking much like English schoolboys from any poor district, with their caps on their heads, their scarves around their necks and their bare knees showing through their open raincoats; then they said their prayers and settled down to study the Bible and the Talmud. They went to the cinema whenever they could; they read comics and exchanged them with one another; they debated about the merits of motor cars; they followed the fortunes of their favourite football teams. But they seldom went to watch football, because most of the games were played on the Sabbath; many of them didn't cut the hair at their temples because that was forbidden by the Law they studied; they didn't buy ice-cream from the carts in the streets because it wasn't kosher; they never took their caps off in class, let alone in the street; they prayed at all odd hours of the day, with antique gestures; they believed literally in every word of the Bible – or tried to believe in every word of it. They were heroic, absurd, and maddening.

I was not a great success as a teacher. I don't think I would have been, anyway, with any boys, because of my youth, my lack of conviction in myself in the role, and my uncertainty about some of the subjects I was supposed to be teaching. And because of my South African accent, which the boys – who themselves spoke with the oddest North London Cockney-Jewish accent – found an unfailing source of amusement and which I used to hear them imitating behind my back. ('Yaw' I'd hear them saying, 'we'll furst do histry; awfter histry, meths.') But what told most against me was that I was, in their eyes, an apostate. Many of them simply refused to believe that I was Jewish; others bombarded me with what they imagined to be penetrating questions. Why didn't I wear a hat, or at least a *kappel*? Did I shave every day? Did I eat pork? Did I go to *shul*? Didn't I believe in God? Wasn't I frightened of what would happen to me, if I went on breaking the Law?

I answered those questions I thought I could answer ('without offence'); I ignored the rest. But they were satisfied neither by my answers nor by my silences. I was always putting my foot wrong, anyway. I interrupted boys at prayer, not knowing that that was what they were doing. I told them to kneel when we were doing a class reading of *Henry IV Part I*, which improbably enough, was their set Shakespeare. ('Sir!' they cried out in horror, 'only *goyim* kneel!') I revealed that I'd been to the theatre on a Friday evening, that I rode on a bus on a Saturday. I wasn't sure of the sequence in which the holy-days came round, and knew the significance of only the more important ones. I had never studied Talmud; I knew little Hebrew (these boys believed it to be sinful to use the language for any but religious purposes); I didn't know the details of the laws of *kashrut*. The boys used to enjoy enlightening and correcting me, they used to enjoy even their own sense of outrage at my lapsed, ignorant state; but their corrections and cries of outrage weren't a help in maintaining discipline.

And yet, somehow, we managed – managed almost as well as anyone else did in the school, I suspect. Its organisation was chaotic; so much so that one could hardly talk of it having any organisation at all. I was never given a syllabus, a time-table, a register; there was a chronic shortage of books and pencils and chalk to write with on the single, scarred blackboard. At irregular intervals – sometimes twice a week, sometimes once a week, and in some weeks not at all – Mr B would come in to give my boys French; the rest of the time I was left to do what I liked with them. We went through the arithmetic books and the geometry primer that they swore they had been through twice already, with other teachers; we worked our way through the English grammar books that some of them seemed to know off by heart. And what books they were – physically, I mean: ancient, coverless, dogeared scraps of things, literally bewhiskered where the stitching along their spines had unravelled, illustrated on every page by schoolboy drawings, held together by glue and scotch tape. They were collected by the 'books monitor' (a position eagerly competed for) at the end of each lesson, and piled in the cupboard, along with the Hebrew books, in rather better condition, which were also stored there, and the unclaimed caps and broken schoolbags thrust into a corner.

There were no geography books, no history books, no science books, no nature-study books; but I was expected to teach them history and geography, nature-study and science, all the same. I was also expected to teach them drawing, though I had no talent at all for drawing. Inevitably, under these circumstances, we spent much of our time simply talking to one another. Or I read them stories. *Treasure Island* was a huge success; it used almost to frighten me, when I would look up and see in their rapt, fixed, hungry eyes, even in the strained tendons of their necks, the effect the book was having on them. *Gulliver's Travels* was much less of a success, I remember, and *Tom Sawyer*, too, was rather a disappointment; they enjoyed many of the details, but the story as a whole didn't hold their attention.

But even in the formal lessons, there were times when I felt that we exchanged something of value with one another; and there were a few boys with whom I felt this often. One I remember with especial fondness was a tall, bespectacled boy with long plump limbs and a mild, indifferent manner, who wrote the best essays in the class, and spelt the most atrociously. I suspected him of being a secret liberal, among all the other young fanatics. But almost any of the boys at one time or another would reveal an unexpected interest, or manage to come out with a genuinely witty remark (they all came out continuously, compulsively, with would-be witty remarks), or would just give a sigh of pleasure at his own insight when some point I was trying to make would suddenly become clear to him, or a sum he was doing would come out, or one fact would remind him of another he hadn't previously connected with it.

There were also a few, of course, with whom it was impossible to make any contact at all. It was humiliating to find that their malice was equal, invariably, to their capacity to enrage. I would tell myself that I would not be provoked by them – next time; that I would respond coolly and effectively to their impertinence or insolence, or to their studied, idle sabotage of the lessons. But at some crucial moment in a lesson, just when I felt I had at least succeeded in rousing the curiosity of the class, one of the malicious ones would let fly with a paper dart, or would start scratching noisily at his desk with a razor blade, or would hold his nose ostentatiously and fan his hand in the air, to indicate to everyone around him that someone had farted. Whereupon I would forget my resolutions and hear my voice rise in rage; hot, embarrassed, and without dignity, I would see the class escape from me in the resulting excitement – whether or not I succeeded in imposing silence on them – and the lesson would be in ruins.

One of the worst offenders was a small, swarthy boy with the longest and most pious earlocks in the class; he used to wear them curled back behind his ears, like the earpieces of a pair of spectacles. Considering his appearance, that boy was altogether a surprise. When the summer came I used to take my class to play cricket, one afternoon a week, in a nearby park, and he proved himself to be a fine batsman, with a natural sense of timing and an elegant way of using his feet. He used to knock my bowling all over the field, much to the pleasure of the others. There was another boy who was an especial torment to me: a twitcher, a liar, a retailer of dirty jokes, a puller of faces. Secretly, I suspected him of being a little mad; I was sure there were times when he gibbered and pulled his faces not in order to annoy me, but simply because he couldn't help himself. I once suggested to Mr B that he should be sent to a child guidance clinic, but the suggestion was received so coldly I did not make it again. Eventually, he was caught chalking the wall that faced the street with the words 'This is a rotten school' in letters twelve inches high. From then on it was agreed, para- doxically enough, that he was indeed a problem case. But, so far as I knew, nothing was ever done about him.

The boys were all poor: the poverty of the school was chronic, irremediable. The signs of poverty I had seen in Mr B's office on my first visit were to be found in the staff-room, which was as long, as bare, and as cluttered with papers as the office, and also in every classroom, in the lavatories and lobbies, in the small asphalted playground at the back. There wasn't a carpet or a bit of linoleum in the place. Every wall was cracked and defaced with scribblings; every window was filthy and every desk battered; every bookcase was split down the sides and was half-filled with books in the same condition as those in my classroom cupboard. The floorboards yielded with a sigh or groan when you stepped on them; the treads of the stairs were worn into so many splintered concavities; the doors hung crooked in their frames and the door-handles turned uselessly in your grasp. There was not a blade of grass in the front garden, not a single piece of equipment in the playground at the back. Even the bat we played cricket with was dry and splintered, like one of those stairs, and the buckles of the pads had long been lost and replaced with bits of string. Black, tubular iron stoves which scorched when you stood near them and gave no warmth when you stepped away from them were the sole source of heating in the school; dusty, unshaded light-bulbs hanging from encrusted pieces of flex provided the only light when the day was overcast. Everything was grey, black, brown, dirty cream – the colours of penury.

Each Friday, soon after lunch, Mr B used to come into my class and call for two or three boys, who owned bicycles and whose parents were regular in their payment of fees, to go out to collect money from parents who had fallen behind. This was done so that the masters could be paid at the end of the afternoon. We always closed a half-hour earlier on Friday afternoons, to give the boys time to get home and wash and change before the Sabbath.

I saw little of the members of the staff on the religious side of the school; they were always leaving the building as I came in, and I never had much occasion to do anything but nod at them as they passed in a succession of black hats, black beards and pale faces. I saw little, too, of the titular head of the school, who was a portly, venerable figure, dressed in the inevitable black hat and black overcoat, but distinguished from the others both by his size and by the whiteness of his beard. He seldom came to the school and could apparently speak very little English. When he did come he depended on Mr B for all the information that came to him. He would nod deeply, with his eyes closed, at the replies Mr B gave to his questions; he would come into the classrooms and tweak the ear of this or that boy, ask the boy's name, and say, 'Good, good, excellent'; from the window of my classroom, I would presently see him make his way out of the school, umbrella clutched firmly, half-way down its length, in his right hand.

Mr B was not only the school secretary; he also taught in the mornings and often in the afternoons as well. Apart from him, the staff teaching secular subjects consisted of one rabbinical student, from Jews' College, two would-be business men, and myself. The would-be business men were both orthodox, but only one of them was successful – the bigger, noisier, better-dressed one. He was in 'the import-export'; that is, an uncle of his who lived in Vienna, and had apparently manufactured the stuff before the war, sent him samples of artificial jewellery, make-up sets, cigarette cases, novelties and trinkets of all kinds, and he went round jewellers' stores, trying to book orders. He had no capital and could carry no stocks, so the building up of his business was a slow job. But his uncle's name was a good one in Vienna, he said, and there were manufacturing firms who were beginning now to let them have credit. He confidently expected to leave off teaching soon, and go into business full-time.

He carried on his business as some demonstrative men carry on their love-affairs. He was always talking about it, or showing us his lines, or boasting to us about the orders he had managed to book, or describing his customers. It would have been unpleasant, had he not been so enthusiastic and naive about it; had he not got so much obvious pleasure from it all. He had pet names for his business, he had little songs about it. I know that must sound unlikely, but it is true. 'Novelties,' he would sing, 'are the life for me/Novelties are the life for you/We will make a fortune from little novelties.' He sang jingles like this in the staff-room, slapping his hands together and sucking his breath between his teeth. He referred to his business when he spoke to us as 'Noveltibirds' or 'Knick-Knack-Novelties' or 'Mickey Marcasite'. Its name on his stationery, however, was exaltedly English in character: something like Marlborough Importers Limited. One lunch-hour, as a great treat, he took me to his office, which was above a row of dingy shops, at the end of a ten-minute bus-ride away from the school. There he pointed out to me his filing cabinet, and his desk; he showed me the samples he kept locked in a cupboard; he ran his fingers like a pianist over his little portable typewriter. 'Nice?' he asked me, as proud as a child. He was by far the happiest man, or boy, at the School.

Poor Y wasn't such a success as a business man. It was because of the apparent success of the other that he too had tried to go into 'the import-export'. He had written to various manufacturers of socks and ties and girls' drawers in Italy, and had asked to be appointed their London agent. One or two had responded, and had sent him samples; on the strength of these he was trying to book orders from clothing and haberdashery stores. But he wasn't doing well. At the end of term, wretchedly embarrassed, he approached me and asked if I would like to buy some of his samples. He showed me what he had of them in his briefcase. I agreed to buy a couple of pairs of green socks. The transaction took place in the staff-room; I can still see Y's small, pale face, with a bush of curly brown hair growing boyishly above it, as he implored me not to tell any of the others about my purchase. He pocketed the money I gave him, and stuffed the socks into a brown paper bag before handing them over to me.

It wasn't really surprising that Y greatly disliked S, the successful one, and used to accuse him of shirking his duties, spying for the school secretary, and thinking of nothing but money. But he never made these accusations in S's presence; instead, they used to have interminable, futile arguments about things they had seen on the television or read in the newspapers. If S had enjoyed a programme, Y said he'd hated it; if S thought the accused in a current murder trial innocent, then Y said he was guilty; if S prophesied a war anywhere on the globe, Y insisted nothing would happen.

The rabbinical student and I were frequently called upon to adjudicate in these disputes; both of us did our best to remain aloof from them. The rabbinical student was invariably quiet in the staff-room. He wore rimless fragile glasses, and had a fluff of gingery beard on his chin; he smiled often, at nothing in particular. I don't think he and I exchanged more than twenty sentences in the months I was at the school. Looking back now, it seems rather strange that none of them showed any particular curiosity about me; they didn't ask me what I was doing in England, or whether I intended making a career out of teaching. At the time I put down their lack of curiosity to the fact that they were all refugees, who had come to England just before or during the war; they were wary of strangers, parsimonious with themselves, anxious not merely to avoid notice but never even to be caught noticing others.

III

Until I came to England it had never really occurred to me that the successive ages and periods of the history text-books could be something other than a sequence of names and numbers which you carried about in your head, like the multiplication tables; I did not know that historical periods could present themselves directly to your vision as you walked about the streets. Now, as I went around London, or made my first solitary forays in the countryside, it seemed to me that the past was something that could actually be seen tapering away from the present, or rather within the present, like a perspective within a picture.

It was self-evident that there should be more Norman than Roman or Anglo-Saxon buildings to be seen; more Gothic than Norman; more Renaissance than Gothic . . . and so on, for century after century, up to the present day. But there they all were, buildings or the ruins of buildings from each of these periods, and the relation they had to one another, in number as well as in appearance, was in itself an historical narrative of a kind, a collective manifestation of the ways in which people had worked and what they had worked at; what they had produced, preserved, inherited; how they had boasted, aspired to excellence, chosen to recognise themselves and compelled others to recognise them. The narrative, in short, was also a style; and the style a tradition. (I could not have imagined then, no one could have imagined, the changes in cityscape and landscape that were to take place over the following decades, and which were to make the perspective I am speaking of seem far more tenuous or dubious than it already was.)

Everything that could be said about the buildings applied also, of course to the institutions housed in them or around them. But then, the British appeared to have the knack not just of closely fitting together their lives and their institutions, but even of turning each into the other. Clubs, pubs, colleges, civil service, schools, trade unions, games, churches, television programmes, the class system, the very characters that individual people had or felt they should have: all provided evidence, one way or another, of this kind of interchangeability. Even the huge green trees in the parks, standing at conversable distances from one another, freighted with leafage and buoyant with the shifting airs of summer, while lovers lay beneath them in motionless disarray – those too looked like more than trees in their places; to my eye they were positively institutional as well.

The country seemed so full, so packed with life, that again and again I couldn't help feeling that if I were merely to close my hand in the air, I would grasp more than air: I would find between my fingers a texture, a colour, a weight.

Once I had settled into my job at the school I used to go much less often to the West End; usually I went in only on Friday evenings, after I'd been paid for my work. When I had been delayed at school I would arrive at Piccadilly Circus or Leicester Square just as the rush-hour began. It used to be part of my Friday evening's entertainment to stand at the foot of the packed escalators of these stations, looking at the crowds descending. Always it seemed as though they were about to topple and fall of their own weight down the steep incline; one felt dizzy standing beneath them, watching the endless chain as it wheeled over with its upright human freight and began its descent. No matter how quickly people stepped from the stairs and hurried away once they had reached the bottom, the wedge on the escalator remained solid, unbroken, it filled entirely the space that was given to it.

Altogether, the London underground was one of the great sights of the city for me. I had never imagined that it would be so complex; that I would spend as much of my time in it as I did; that it would dispose of such huge numbers of people; that it would have its own architecture, its own light, air, smells and noises, and would impose upon the people who travelled in it a characteristic expression of the face; that the stations would be so much alike and yet differ so much from one another, and from themselves at different times of the day. In fact, while I was still unfamiliar with it – before it became merely commonplace, an indifferent and occasionally uncomfortable passage through which I had to make my way so many times a week – the underground seemed to me a symbol or image of a kind that was all the more portentous for being so obscure. It was impossible for me to keep out of my mind all sorts of half-ideas about purgatory and the after-life, as I bewilderedly made my way through one subterranean tunnel to the next, among the hurrying crowds, bent upon their own destinations. At the same time, the underground appeared to be the true centre or source of the city's life, rather than an image of its death. One felt inside it, more so than anywhere else, as though London were nothing but a great machine, contracting and expanding to its own deep, mechanical rhythms; a machine which the people who lived in London did not control but merely had to obey. So they were brought together and hurled apart again, as the machine dictated.

But even to think of the machine 'dictating' to the anonymous crowds made it seem too personal. The machine itself did not know what it was doing: it merely flashed its lights, moved its stairs, sent its trains hurtling along grey, ribbed tunnels, festooned with cables; its servants cried out 'Mind the gap' above the sigh of closing doors and the shuffling sound of the passengers' feet, above the thunderous fading roar of other trains in other tunnels. Sometimes the machine breathed in gales that cut through one's clothing, at other times the air hung still and oppressively warm; there were trains that stopped in mid-tunnel and waited, in a humming and shivering silence, before they moved again; at times the platforms and escalators were deserted, yet the trains still emerged and departed, the stairs continued to rattle and fold in and out of each other. All this vast activity and movement seemed to serve no purpose but that of its own continuation, could not serve any other purpose, for there appeared to be no consciousness that guided or directed it.

I used to wonder, at first, why there were so few literary references to the underground; before I learned to take it for granted, I wondered why everyone else did. In fact, there was one writer I knew of who had used it in his work, and it is partly for this reason, and not only because of what he wrote about the City and its river, about its churches and canals, that T. S. Eliot has remained for me pre-eminently the poet of London; as much London's poet as Dickens is still its novelist.

On these Friday evenings, I would emerge from the underground station and make straight for the theatre of my choice. I would book a stool in the gallery queue, and then try to fill in the time that remained until the theatre opened. Usually, I just walked around the West End and Soho, and looked at shop windows and people, or grubbed among the second-hand books which were then still to be found in the Charing Cross Road, or went a few times to the National Gallery; I ate some kind of a meal and returned to the theatre always in good time. Often enough I was glad to get into it simply to rest my feet.

The cocooned, cosy plush and gilt of the theatres, their ornate chandeliers and braided, pink light-shades in clusters here and there on the walls, were novelties and yet familiar from the descriptions I had read of them; they were 'sights' in much the same way as the faces of the actors and actresses I had seen previously only on the cinema screen. As much as when I walked in the streets, I was sightseeing at the theatre. But this was not the only reason why I went so regularly. I hoped earnestly to discover in myself a passion for the theatre of the kind I had so often read about. It goes almost without saying that I can now hardly remember a single one of the plays I saw; hardly a title, a plot, a joke, a stage-setting. All I can remember are my own efforts to persuade myself into an enthusiasm I was never really able to feel.

Of course, I hoped also that up there in the gallery I would meet some beautiful, young, sincere, lonely, ardent, female theatre-lover, and that a friendship, and more than a friendship, would develop between us. The closest I came to it, however, was to see several times at various theatres a quite pretty girl, who grew to recognise me, and who I think would have welcomed an approach from me. What held me back was that this girl was always accompanied by her youthful and goodlooking mother – which was something my fantasies had never bargained for. I couldn't possibly tackle them both, of that I was sure; so the girl and I never did more than exchange a few uncertain smiles.

In the novels I read, young men in the position I was in were continually picking up attractive girls in streets and parks and bookshops; I had no such luck. As a matter of fact, of the loners I have since met in London, only one man has seemed able to do it again and again. He found his girls for the most part in coffee-bars, which weren't in existence my first year in London, and in museums, which at that time I did not much frequent. But I doubt if I'd have been much more successful even if coffee-bars had been in existence and had I made a habit of visiting museums more often. I hadn't the knack. All I did have was a host of images of the girl I would eventually meet. Sometimes she was English, sometimes South African; sometimes she was tall, sometimes slight; sometimes she was dark, sometimes fair; sometimes she was sophisticated, sometimes naive; invariably, she was generous, high-spirited, and compliant. But because I was without friends, visited no homes, went to no parties, it seemed that I had no chance of meeting her – though all too often I would catch a glimpse of her, in a crowd of other girls, or on the arm of another man.

Always, everywhere, I felt myself to be touched, nudged, pulled by the sexual underworld of London; an underworld much wider than that of the whores who then used to stand on every West End corner after nightfall, or of the homosexuals hanging about outside the men's lavatories in Leicester Square and Trafalgar Square tube-stations. These the newspapers wrote about every other weekend; but they never said a word about the furtive encounters and withdrawals that took place in darkened, half-empty cinemas; about the rubber-shops with their dangling trusses, books on flagellation, and their offers to send you 'further literature' in 'plain wrappers'; about the wild, imploring graffiti scribbled upon the doors and walls of practically every public lavatory; about the packed tube-trains, where the crowds swayed promiscuously against one another, heads respectably averted, bodies rammed together. Or, for that matter, about the sedate, secluded middle-class house in which I lodged, and in which almost every room seemed filled with whispers that sometimes rose to cries, behind the closed doors, sniggers, sobs, expostulations.

I knew none of the people who lodged in the house; we passed each other on the stairs, and greeted one another, and that was all.

Yet it surprises me now to realise just how much I did learn about them; at least about those who lived on my landing. There was, for example, the Danish student (so-called: he was much older in appearance than any student had the right to be) in the room next door to mine. His girl spent one week in his room crying almost continuously, and then left for Australia: that I guessed from the silence which descended upon his room when the week was over, and from the Australian air-letters addressed to him, in a feminine hand, which shortly afterwards began to appear on the window-ledge where the housekeeper left all our letters. Had she always planned to go to Australia? Had she threatened to go to Australia unless he married her? Or was she Australian, and had she wept simply because she had to go home and he wouldn't follow? In any case, the Scandinavian did not pine for her. The last girl had cried; his new one laughed. I would hear the deep, gurgling sound of her laughter at all hours of the night – above the sound of Radio Luxembourg, to which the radio in that room seemed to be permanently tuned.

The room next to mine on the other side was occupied by an elderly German Jewish widow, whose daughter, I gathered from overheard snatches of conversation in German and English, was unhappily married. The daughter complained to her mother about her husband's stinginess with money, his angry moods, his absences; the mother counselled patience. I saw the husband a few times on the stairs: a tall, fair, high-coloured man, with the face of a disgruntled boy. To judge from his accent, he too was a German Jew, but he always spoke in English. He had almost as many complaints against his wife as she had against him; what was very odd about his way of delivering these complaints was that he seemed to take it for granted that his mother-in-law would agree with him. 'She's impossible, isn't she?' he would say to his mother-in-law at the end of some story about her daughter, or, 'What can you do with someone like that, tell me, please.' These familial confrontations took place about once a week (the daughter came three or four times a week), and usually ended up with the three of them going at the mother's suggestion, to the pictures.

Across the landing there lived the quietest of the couples on my floor: a tall well-spoken Englishman in his middle thirties, who went off every morning in a dark suit and bowler hat to the bank or insurance office in which he worked, and his small, curly-headed youthful Cypriot boy-friend. The youngster was apparently supported by his friend and seldom went out. He used to potter about the house, and have long conversations with the housekeeper, and listen to the soap-operas on the radio. When he did go out he wore clothes of a very different kind from those of his friend; striped shirts, black jeans, belts with big silver buckles. The two of them seemed staid and settled, and I shall never know why the Englishman suddenly left; certainly, there had been no loud rows before his departure.

It must have been just two or three days after the Englishman had left that the young man knocked on my door. He had come with a suggestion, or an invitation. Wouldn't I move in with him? We had never done more than greet one another, as I have said, or exchange a few remarks about the weather. Now he stood with his back against the wall, a pace away from the door, and smiled at me guilelessly. 'It's a fine room,' he said. 'It's too dear for me. But with you – with the two of us – it'd be easy.' And he made a gesture with his hand, twisting the palm of it open, towards me. The invitation, and the gesture which accompanied it, seemed somehow both obscene and touching. Still he smiled; he was a round-cheeked, brown-eyed boy, with white teeth and dark curls that fell all over his forehead. I wondered what it was about me that had made him think I might be a suitable successor to his English friend, 'No, thank you,' I said. 'It's kind of you to ask me, but – '

Nevertheless he persisted. He invited me to come and look at the room which was much bigger than the one I had. He would keep it clean, cook, look after everything. So I told him (untruthfully) that I was preparing for an examination, I studied in the evenings, and couldn't possibly consider sharing with anyone.

'Oh,' he assured me, his smile even more artless than before, 'I can be very quiet.'

This time I simply shook my head in silence. My gaze, I'm sure, was far more embarrassed than the one with which he met it. But he was very polite; almost condescending. He shrugged, said he hoped I didn't mind that he'd asked me, and slid out of the room. A few days later he was gone. His room was then occupied by a couple of girl-students, one of whom I thought attractive in a soft, eager, earnest, innocent way. Even when you know nothing about them or their circumstances, girls like that somehow make you feel that you should sympathise with their views and admire their pluck. I looked forward to meeting her on the stairs; when we did meet I tried to make our conversation last as long as possible. The development of our friendship was cut short by an unfortunate accident, however. All the people on my landing shared a single, huge bathroom-cum-lavatory. One afternoon I opened the door of this room, and there, on the lavatory seat, sat this girl, with her pants around her ankles. She had forgotten to lock the door behind her. For the briefest and most protracted of seconds we stared at one another; then she gave a kind of moan, and reached down towards her ankles, while I retreated, muttering apologies and banging the door closed behind me.

From then on the poor girl couldn't say a word to me. When she saw me she blushed, she ducked, she scurried away down the passage or up the stairs. As long as I lived in the house she never forgave me, or herself, for what had happened.

The story I had told the Cypriot about working for an examination had been untrue. But it was true that I was working almost every evening, at this time. I had begun writing, in earnest – or so I thought. At any rate, what drove me to start working seemed to me earnest enough.

I was still seeing the K's and G and his girl friend, on alternate weeks; in addition there was a girl I had known at university in Johannesburg whom I saw even more infrequently; there were friends of K and G with whom I spent occasional evenings. Generally, this meant that in every week I was in the company of others one evening or perhaps one weekend afternoon; the other six nights, the rest of the weekends, I was on my own. I was no longer able to fill them, as I had been able to at first, simply by being on the move.

Loneliness had had its pleasures; there had been something extraordinarily satisfying, at times, in the thought that none of the people who ever saw me knew who I was; conversely, there was a kind of exhilaration in the thought that at any given moment none of the people who did know me could guess just where I was, what I was doing, where I would go next. But I found that these moments of excitement or self-satisfaction were recurring less and less frequently. Also, I had begun to have fears that were worse than the mild hallucinations or displacements that I had been afflicted with in my first few weeks in the city, when again and again, in broad daylight, I had found myself thinking I was back in Johannesburg, or had made a habit of 'recognizing' people who in fact were complete strangers to me. Chiefly, I was afraid now of falling ill or having an accident. 'It could be weeks before anyone would even know!' – that seemed to be the real horror of the situation.

Actually, I was exaggerating the forlorness of my own position. Now that I was working, any absence of mine would certainly have been noticed; and, after a very few days Mr B would have gone over to the nursery department of the school (which was run, by the way, quite independently from his) and would have asked Naomi what had happened to me. And Naomi would, I am sure, have taken the trouble to come to my room to find out. But what could she have done for me if she did come? What if I wasn't there? What if I was in some hospital, miles away – unconscious, perhaps? It didn't occur to me that in that case I would then be unconscious of my own loneliness as well; but I doubt if the thought would have been of much comfort. Nor did I find it much of a comfort to remind myself that my health had so far been excellent, and showed no signs of deteriorating suddenly.

Still, it is always easy to be superior to one's own anxieties when one no longer feels them; the truth is that if I had fallen ill I would probably have had a thoroughly miserable time of it. In the best of health, I was finding my loneliness quite heavy enough a burden, anyway. It was at this time, I remember, that the notices which used to be posted up outside Tottenham Court Road police station began to have a macabre fascination for me. 'Found: in Thames, near Greenwich, body of man, aged 20–23, wearing brown sports jacket and grey flannels, height 5′ 7″, scar on right cheek . . .' 'Found: 63 – Crescent, N.W., body of woman, aged 50 years approx . . .' To prevent such a notice ever being posted up about me, I wrote my name and parents' address in South Africa on a piece of paper, and put it in my wallet. It embarrassed me to do this, I remember; but I did it, nevertheless.

So I stayed in my room more than ever before; I felt safer there than anywhere else. Because I had to do something to fill in these phobic hours, I began to write a novel. However, if I began work on it as a means of self-defence, it was not long before I thought of the book as a means of attack; as the instrument through which I might be able to subdue the city beyond the walls of the room. I had no precise idea of what London would look like to me once it was subdued; but I was sure, at least, that it would seem a very different place from what it had been hitherto. Months later I finished the novel, and was glad to put it quietly out of sight.

One afternoon I came home early from school – I forget why – and found a little girl waiting on the doorstep. She had come for her dancing lesson (the ground floor of the house was still occupied by the school of dancing). While I looked through my pockets for my key she told me that her daddy had brought her in his car, and that he was going to fetch her when the lesson was over. She said she'd been ringing at the door-bell but no one had answered it.

At the time I wasn't struck by the oddity of this. Usually, on afternoons when lessons were held in the house, the front door was simply left wide open. I cannot remember what the little girl looked like, except that she had freckles on her face, and that like all the little girls who came for their classes she carried her dancing-shoes in a small cloth bag. What I do recall was that her voice was sweet and clear, and that I was touched by the volubility with which she chattered to me during the minute or two we stood together on the step. As it happened, I really had to hunt for my key, in every pocket, before I finally found it. Then I opened the door. As I did it, I felt rather pleased with myself for having been able to help her. Once we were inside I simply went straight up the stairs, and she very politely called after me, from the big, gloomy lobby of the house, 'Good-bye. Thank you.' I replied to her without looking back.

How long it was before she called to me again, I cannot now say. Indeed, in many ways the whole incident has the quality of a bad dream; except that I know, to my regret, that it wasn't a dream, that it actually happened. I think that I settled down to read, once I was in my room, or perhaps I just lay on my bed; in any case, I remained awake. It seems almost unbelievable to me now that I could have sat or lain there, in that dead-silent house, without thinking that something was amiss. But I know quite well how I was able to do it. I had simply forgotten about the little girl; I had smiled at her, and listened to her chatter, and opened the door for her, and then she had just gone out of my mind, as though I had never seen her. So much so that I did not even think of her when I heard a child's voice calling out, of all things, 'I'm only seven.'

I thought the call came from somewhere outside in the street; it struck me as rather a strange thing for a child to shout out, but I assumed it was some part of a game or an argument. Afterwards, that first call struck me as being as pitiful as anything that followed; it showed so clearly how the girl's own puniness, in that enormous, silent house, must have been borne in upon her. But I wasn't thinking of her, then. That first call was followed by a long silence, and then by a shriek as terrified, and therefore as terrifying, as any I have ever heard. 'Mister man! Help me! I don't know my way home! You're my friend!' A moment later the front door shut with a bang that shook the entire house.

Only then, when it was too late, I realized that the voice was that of the little girl that I had let into the house; that it was to me she had been calling. I knew at once what had happened; I should have known before I had opened the door which should not have been closed; I should certainly have known when I had left her in that still, empty lobby. There was no dancing lesson that afternoon; it had been cancelled for some reason, and her parents had either not been told or had forgotten, and had dropped her at the gate as usual. Then I had let her in. There was not a soul in the house apart from myself; by some mischance everyone was out – the housekeeper, the widow, the girl students, everyone. The little girl had sat alone in the half-darkness, and waited, and waited, until terror had overwhelmed her. But she had not forgotten me as I had forgotten her; she had cried out to me, telling me that she was only seven; again she had waited, until there had come that shriek, that appeal to me as her friend; then, before I could do anything, she had fled from the house.

Her friend! The one who had brought her into the house, and had ignored her first cry for help! I was down the stairs in an instant, and out in the street. I looked up the slope of the hill; there was no one to be seen that way. The distance the other way, down to the Finchley Road, was only about fifty yards; I was sure she must have made for it, though I could not see her. I ran down to the corner. It was hopeless. The pavements of Finchley Road were crowded with people, throngs of them, advancing and retreating, pausing, hurrying forward, turning aside; in the road itself trucks ground their gears, moved forward, stood idle, their exhaust fumes rising in the air. There wasn't a sign of the little girl. I ran half a block in one direction, turned and ran back in the other. She was gone, lost in the crowd. In the months that followed I looked for her many times, when the children gathered in groups outside the house before or after their lessons, but she was never among them.

IV

Not long after that episode, the circumstances in which I was living in London changed greatly. For one thing, I lost my job at the school in a manner which seemed to me quite farcical. The boys had set a trap for me, and I had walked right into it. 'Please sir,' they asked in innocent tones during a history lesson, 'how old is the world?' 'Oh, millions of years,' I answered blithely. 'Millions and millions of years.' No sooner had the words been said than an unwonted hush fell on the class. A score of hot, accusing eyes were fixed on me. Then uproar broke out. 'Sir, you believe that men come from monkeys! Sir, you don't believe that God made the world! Sir, it says in the Bible how old the world is! Sir – ! Sir – ! Sir – !'

This assault did not upset or even bother me much. I told them to shut up ('Some people believed one thing; some people believed another') and dragged them unwillingly back to the subject we had been talking about before. It was plain that the question had been carefully staged; but that in itself was not enough to make me attach any importance to the incident. Within a couple of days I had forgotten about it. So I was surprised to receive shortly afterwards a letter from Mr B in which a month's notice was given to me. This was being done, the letter said, because parents had complained of what I had been telling the children about the Bible in my classes. Naturally I took the letter to Mr B's office and challenged him with it. Then it came out. I had denied the truth of the Biblical account of the creation of the universe. I had been teaching the doctrine of evolution. Thus I had finally managed to give offence, as Mr B had originally warned me against doing.

Since the only emotion his letter had roused in me, apart from surprise, was that of relief at the prospect of being compelled to leave the school, I made no protestations of innocence. When he had finished I told him exactly what had happened – not, as I made clear, because I wished to remain in the school – but because I owed it to myself to do so. Mr B listened carefully to my tale. He not only listened to it, he believed it. 'You know,' he said, 'they caught just such a one as you with the same question a couple of years ago.'

The term ended and my notice expired on the same day. I had no idea what I would do after the holiday. It was hard for me to believe, though, that any of the boys could have been as delighted to be shut of the place as I was. I would have been even more delighted if I had known that the isolation I had been living in was suddenly, for a variety of reasons unconnected with one another, about to come to an end.

The whole experience of coming to London and living alone in it for those months had left me with a series of questions which were to become as intimately a part of me as my memories. When I looked back at South Africa, the country of my birth, it seemed to me not only flat and bare, not only given over to the political and social torments peculiar to it, but also haphazard, unformed, flat; the very faces of the people, I now thought, were lacking in depth and subtlety, their voices empty of resonance. English society, in all its embodiments and manifestations, was incomparably more elaborate than anything I had dreamed of before. Space itself seemed denser in England, used more intensively to a greater variety of purposes; the same was true of time, even in its passage from season to season, not to speak of the freight from the past it carried with it.

Well, what difference did this make? Or rather: why did it make such a difference to me? To the east there were countries as ancient, as dense socially, as England, where a few years before people were murdered in their millions simply because they came of the same stock as myself. My grandparents and parents had literally saved their lives by migrating from Europe to South Africa. Where then, did that leave the advantages supposedly to be derived from living among ancient buildings and great works of art and other such residues of the past? How could I reconcile my own family history with the delight I took in that congruence between the written word and the visible world which Europe had always taken for granted, and which unadorned, undescribed South Africa lacked?

History and art both pretended to be so much more than spectacles or diversions; they hinted at meanings, purposes, revelations, conclusions. But the one stumbled blindly from event to event; the other proferred us modes of self-comprehension which appeared to have no discernible effect on the way we actually behaved to one another or how we felt about ourselves. Then what was the good of them? Of having their accumulations around us? What help did they give us? And if these were inappropriate questions to ask, what would be the right ones?

Looking back, it seems easy to say that even in asking such questions I was irrevocably committing myself to living in England. It did not feel like that then. Everything then was provisional, doubtful, tentative, and was felt all the more intensely for being so. I had ambitions but no plans; yearnings but no object for them. The amplitude and the opacity of the future were one.

FATE, ART,
LOVE, AND GEORGE

One day a young man I had never spoken to before, and was never to speak to again, asked me a question. I answered it as best I could; he thanked me and a few minutes later left the room. The name of that young man was George. He intervened in my life as decisively as anyone I have ever met. Yet his name is almost all I know about him. Not only was I never to speak to him again, I was never to see him thereafter, never to hear anything about him in any context whatever. It was as if (for me) he existed solely to open his mouth, change my life, and then vanish.

Not that either of us knew he was going about the business of fate when he approached me. If fate had a plot or plan for me it could be fulfilled only through my ignorance of what was to come: or, to put it another way, through my seeking as earnestly as I could to fulfil my own plots and plans. And of course by George seeking to fulfil his.

The brief meeting between us took place in Kimberley. George, who was about the same age as myself, had gone to a 'rival', Catholic, high school, and as a result we had repeatedly played rugby against one another. That was how I knew his name – I had heard his team-mates shout it out – and why his firm features, black eyes, dark brows, and strikingly contrasted fair curls were familiar to me. After leaving school I had gone to university in Johannesburg; then, before going overseas for the first time, I had returned to Kimberley, intending to spend a few weeks with my parents. But I had been trapped at home because my father had fallen seriously ill. Since I had little to do while I waited for his recovery, I used to go often to the public library. On this particular afternoon George, who had apparently never left Kimberley, came up to me in the smoking room of the library and asked if I had been at college the past few years. When I said yes, he then asked me, as if I were bound to be an authority on the subject, which of the country's universities he would best be advised to apply to, in order to study economics.

How could I tell? Economics was a subject I knew nothing about. I said so. Simply for politeness' sake, I added something about the two biggest universities in the country, in Cape Town and Johannesburg, probably being the best in all the subjects they offered. I said no more to him. He said no more to me. At that point we were interrupted by someone I had not seen before, who had been sitting in an armchair with its back to us; he had been so deeply sunken into the chair that not even the top of his head had been visible. Perhaps he could be of help, he said; he'd done some courses in economics at Rhodes University, in Grahamstown, and he could tell George something about the way the subject was taught there

So he and George went into a corner and talked earnestly to one another. The Kimberley public library in those days was more like a gentleman's club than any library I have seen since. Erected in Victorian times, it contained many smallish, oddly shaped, secluded rooms which were equipped with buttoned leather armchairs and leather-topped tables, creaking bookcases (some with tall glass doors), framed portraits of civic and military dignitaries, open fireplaces, ticking clocks, chess boards, spiral staircases of cast iron, and other such luxuries. The smoking room was so much like a gentleman's club, in fact, as to be a 'men only' room: it was the most secluded, the most leathery, the least-frequented of the lot; immediately outside it was a shady verandah and access to no less than two gardens, one of which was dominated by an expansive jacaranda tree. I had never before seen George in that room, or anywhere else in the library; the man he was talking to was even more of a stranger. After a discussion between the two of them lasting perhaps five minutes, George left the room with a wave of the hand to me. He had done his duty. He had done enough for me to have reason to remember that encounter for as long as I will be able to remember anything.

Now it was the stranger's turn. He approached me diffidently, yet with the hungrily expectant air of a man who was not going to let the chance of striking up a conversation go by. His face was clever and bony, his nose was sharp, his accent and intonation more cultivated than those ordinarily heard in Kimberley. He was a few years older than I was. The irony or diffidence of his manner, and the watchfulness of his gaze, did not conceal his appetite for speech. On the contrary, they made it more apparent. He referred awkwardly to George's enquiry and to my cautious response to it. So we got talking to one another. It turned out that he was indeed a stranger to the town, as I had surmised; that he had been employed for the past few months in the bureaucracy responsible for managing one of the black 'locations' on the outskirts of town; that he lived in a hotel room in a dismal suburb not far from my home; that aside from the people in his office, none of whom he had found congenial, he had met nobody since his arrival; that as a result he was bitterly lonely, bored, and dejected. It also turned out that at some of the national students' gatherings he had attended he had met one or two people whom I had known slightly in Johannesburg; and that I had actually seen him perform in a Rhodes University production of T. S. Eliot's *Murder in the Cathedral* which had come to the campus in Johannesburg during the previous year.

After some time we left the cool shadows and gleaming reflections of the library and went out to face the glare of the street. We were in the middle of town, but, since it was a Saturday afternoon, the weekend vacancy was already on it. Helpless with boredom, stupefied by their own nullity, town and sky yawned at one another. Old buildings two storeys high, with elaborate fronts, alternated with garish new buildings four or five storeys high. Nobody looked at the dresses or cars or electrical equipment displayed in their ground-floor windows. There were no other pedestrians to be seen and no cars on the roadway. The only movement was that of the sunlight glittering off everything it touched – glass, metal, asphalt. We took refuge in a milk-bar and continued our conversation there. I had grown up in Kimberley, I was living at home, I knew by name and sight hundreds of people in the town, yet after having been away I felt cut off from the place; just as I felt it to be cut off from the world. So it was hard for me to imagine how the stranger (Owen, his name was) endured his evenings and weekends in the Phoenix Hotel, Beaconsfield. No doubt he stared across the railway line and the sandy wastes of the Beaconsfield market square, and over the corrugated iron fences, tumbledown shops, and vacant spaces littered with paper and orange peels which were to be seen in the other direction. And then?

Well, he read a lot. He wrote to his girl friend, in Rhodesia, who was supposed to be joining him in a couple of months' time. Having got that far, he ran out of explanations of how he spent his leisure and simply shrugged despairingly. Given our respective situations, it is not surprising that we soon decided, as we sat there, that we had quite a lot in common. We had read some of the same books. We both intended to go abroad as soon as we could. We recognised each other with some relief, and more than a touch of complacency, as members of that freemasonry of enlightened, superior spirits who saw the country's social and racial arrangements not only as a misfortune on a vast scale, but also as a grotesque joke. However, what we had most in common, I now suspect, was a feeling shared by all ambitious, young provincials: the feeling that they are living in disguise in their own homeland; that they are positively disfigured by their surroundings, compelled to conceal their deepest natures from themselves and from everyone else; and that all this is going to be changed soon, somehow, elsewhere.

In due course, Owen got married, left Kimberley, and went to live in England. I followed him there, by a circuitous route, later. Once I was settled in London, Owen and his wife invited me to visit them in a little cottage they had rented in Yorkshire. By then he had a junior appointment in a university nearby. He had thus begun the career in the English academic establishment which was eventually to lead him, through all the appropriate stages, to a professorship, a headship of department, the membership of various professional committees, the publication of several books on social theory. In the meantime, coping with the bleak Yorkshire spring, he and his wife lived in chilly, skimpy circumstances. They were not alone in their cottage: partly because it was so crowded, I stayed there for a few days only. There was a couple with a child staying with them, and a young woman with a baby, who was on her own. This young woman planned to come to London later in the year, to start a course at London University. She and I did not have much to say to one another during my stay; but before I left she asked me if I would help her find accommodation in London in the autumn. I promised, without much conviction, to do what I could for her.

One consequence of that conversation was that she and I kept in touch; a consequence of that, in turn, was that we eventually became lovers and started living together in a flat in Highgate belonging to a certain Miss Bunbury. The flat was an unusual place, in an unusual situation, as I shall describe shortly. Our affair was somewhat unusual too, in that it was hedged about with *a priori* rules of our own devising. We lived together only at weekends. We prided ourselves on not making demands of each other at other times. We insisted that the arrangement was nothing more than a mutually convenient one which could be terminated at the will of either party. Each of us declared that we had every intention of terminating it at some time still to be decided on. Etcetera.

None of these understandings proved to be workable or durable. It did not take long, no more than a couple of months, for that to become apparent to us both. Winter months they were, and a bitterly cold winter too; so cold that the vapour from our commingled breath froze every Saturday and Sunday night on the inside of the window-glass of the bedroom we shared. Outside, heavy trucks heading north would get into their lowest gear to grind up the Archway Road: a sound which affected one as an unlocalised or indefinable physical pressure, something one became fully aware of or could identify only after it had come to its end, when the truck reached the top of the hill and changed gear.

Aside from the noise, though, one would never have known that the flat was part of a terrace just yards from the main road. Surrounded by trees and by banks of earth, it could not be seen from the road and the road could not be seen from it. Access was provided only by secretive flights of steps: one at the back, which came straight down from the iron bridge over the road; the other at the end of a narrow alleyway which ran at right angles to the road and took yet another right angled turn before the steps began. Then one came suddenly on this group of houses, built of ruddy bricks, surmounted by cosy, Dutchified gables, adorned with white-sashed windows. The flat itself had been Miss Bunbury's own residence before she had let it, and the furnishings consisted of a plethora of battered wardrobes, chests of drawers, sofas, armchairs, hatstands, standing lamps, fireguards, coal scuttles and so forth. When I had first seen it, some of the walls and door-frames had been festooned with pinned-up pages torn from ancient newspapers: on these pages advertisements from the 'Personal' columns had been encircled in red. They were thus mute witnesses to other lives which Miss Bunbury had dreamed of living. She might have been a companion and housekeeper to an elderly Englishman with a house in Spain. A member of a small, select group intending to spend several weeks in Greece, followed by a month in Egypt. A friend to a cultivated lady in Somerset (car-driver essential).

Actually, Miss Bunbury was a woman of means. It would never have occurred to me to think of her in such terms then; but it does now. She was a disorderly, dishevelled, soft-faced, open-mouthed, grey-haired spinster, who wore dim layers of garments over a broad but wholly featureless body, and carried hessian bags, stuffed with a variety of goods and papers, in both hands. On her stout calves were stockings drawn up no higher than her knees, and kept in place by garters under the rolls of lisle or cotton which she had made surplus to her requirements. She looked more like a beggar-woman than a recently retired schoolteacher, and more like a re-tired schoolteacher than a woman of property. But she was both of the latter. I have forgotten where she had done her teaching; but I could go straight to the properties she owned. The one in High-gate consisted of the entire house at the end of the terrace, and not just the flat I have described; the other, in Swiss Cottage, was an even more substantial affair, which was also divided into rooms and flats to let.

Picture Miss Bunbury, then, coming at her own request to the Highgate flat one Saturday morning. Her bags are full and her clothes dishevelled, as usual; she wears a round felt hat, squashed down to beret-like proportions, over her stiff grey hair. She has come to change the curtains in the living room. For some arcane reason faded green velvet is to be changed to faded orange floral print. Or vice versa. Much measuring and clambering about takes place as a result: some of it is done by her, which reveals her stock-ings and the copious, shadowy, naked thighs above; some of it is done by me, under the *nom de guerre* of 'David', which is what Miss Bunbury insists on calling me. I move chairs, hold up lengths of curtaining, lean rods against walls. On the other side of suddenly exposed, grimy windows, the winter sun shines down. My friend makes tea and then goes out to do some shopping. I retire to the kitchen table to try to do some work of my own. Miss Bunbury declines the offer of a light lunch; she contents herself with more tea and biscuits. She is evidently in no hurry to get the work done. She stitches here, snips away there. For this one morning, it seems, and then for a good part of the afternoon, we are in effect replacing that gentleman in the south of Spain, that cultivated lady in Somer-set, by providing her with a little company. Finally, as the sunlight contracts, grows paler, loses discernible outline, fades into the ground like water being swallowed up, Miss Bunbury repacks her bags in order to admit the curtains she has taken down, puts on her hat and a thick, dark overcoat, and waddles off through the front door.

The bags weigh her down. It will be a long journey for her, on foot and by underground train, back to Swiss Cottage, where she now lives. Half-hidden behind the newly hung curtains, we stand in the living room, amid the furniture she owns, and watch her go down the garden path. Now she has reached the first of the flights of steps that will take her down to the road. There, while the half-light seems to erode her figure moment by moment, and true darkness winks at us out of the moving leaves and branches above her, she comes to a halt. She puts down her bags. Exhausted already? No, she has something else in mind. She proceeds to rummage in her bags, first in the one, then in the other. Evidently she believes herself to be unobserved. It turns out that what she has been looking for is a bottle of milk. She puts the bottle to her lips, tilts her head back, and drinks ravenously from it. Safe behind the window, buttressed by all the years we have yet to live, we look on in a state of mirthful despair, or delighted pity, at the awfulness of old age, the shamelessness of spinsterhood, the squalor of loneliness, the unimaginable condition of being Miss Bunbury.

Do you believe in fate? Do I? Did Miss Bunbury? If everything that happens to us *is* our fate, then perhaps one can say only that some of it happens because we wish it to happen (even if we may realise this only belatedly or retrospectively or never at all), and that some of it simply happens, beyond our knowledge or will; beyond ourselves, as it were. As I write this, a man approaching the age Miss Bunbury must have been then, I am still living with the woman to whom Miss Bunbury rented her flat – though we parted after that episode, and spent several years at great distances from one another before coming together again. Miss Bunbury did little more for us than to make her flat available at a rent of four pounds ten shillings a week, but she and her flat, its situation, its furniture, its curtains, its newspaper clippings, its sounds, its seclusion, can never be dislodged from that part of our lives; nor, therefore, from what came after.

As for Owen – whom I have seen only twice since I visited him in his cottage: once to talk to briefly, and once to wave to, after a wary exchange of glances from one escalator passing another in a London Underground station – his case is quite different. Consider the circumstances. He was the only person my wife and I knew in common before we met; our circles of acquaintance did not overlap at any other point; only through him was it possible for us to come to know of one another's existence. Yet he and I would never have met if George had not been in the smoking room of the Kimberley public library that particular afternoon, and if he had not spoken to me, out of the blue, for the first and last time in his life. Small though Kimberley was, Owen and I never ran into one another accidentally at any other social occasion during the brief period we were both living in the city. Without George's intervention I would never so much as have seen him and my life would have been unutterably different.

Unutterably? Surely, a sceptic might say, you would probably have decided to live in England, anyway; you would probably have become a writer; you would probably have married; perhaps you would have stayed married; you would probably have had children. . . . But fate, like art, knows nothing of abstractions or generalisations; it has its force, its meaning, its felt presence, only in and through the details of which it is composed; if those details are ultimately inseparable from one another, it is not only because they accumulate relentlessly to make up a whole, but also because each of them in itself seems to contain or express something of that whole. And fate and art, in these respects at least, can be said to be like love, which also feasts on particularities, on details so fleeting and yet so distinctive that they seem to embody the whole person and everything about him or her one loves: a glance, a timbre of the voice, a movement of the brow, a hesitation, a pressure, a texture. Does one love because of them? Or is one aware of them only because one loves?

F. R. LEAVIS

In the privacy of his mind, every young writer probably appoints one or two older writers to whom he turns for support and guidance; authorities to whom he gives an allegiance all the more unqualified because he has himself elevated them to the position they occupy. In my own case, one of the writers whom I had appointed to be a mentor of this kind was F. R. Leavis, the Cambridge critic, teacher, and editor, whose work I first read a couple of years after leaving university. Leavis was of course a passionately controversial figure in the world of English letters: famous both as an enemy of 'Bloomsbury' and the 'London literary establishment' and as a quasi-prophetic denouncer of nothing less than 'industrial civilisation' as a whole. He was also a compellingly delicate and incisive critic of individual poems and novels, and a combative champion of major English authors, like George Eliot and D. H. Lawrence, whose work he felt had been neglected or misunderstood.

For me there was something else at stake in my admiration for his work; something I would not have been able to describe then as I do now. What Leavis offered in his criticism was a model or ideal community which anyone, any reader, could bring into existence without ever stirring from his room. Anyone – his writings seemed to suggest – who read a novel or a poem, and responded wholeheartedly to it, was in effect meeting the novelist or poet in a 'place' which existed *for both of them*, for the writer as much as the reader, nowhere but in the shared experience of the novel or poem. Such a meeting of writer and reader within the work itself, which was the possession of neither and both, constituted the primary community through which a literature came into being. However, that primary community was both the product and the living instance of the larger community of writers and readers, past and present, whose joint efforts constantly recreated the literary tradition as a whole. And that tradition – not seen as so many books or texts external to oneself, 'out there', established *a priori*, but rather felt as a series of inward experiences which had become part of one's own mind, and indeed of one's own body – that tradition was in turn the product and the living instance of the society at large, of its language and history and institutions, domestic and political alike. (Religious believers of all denominations would probably have no difficulty in thinking of the relationships, living in time and through individuals, and yet embodying something beyond time and the individual, which I am trying to describe.) Thus, in Leavis's hands, such concepts as the 'correction of taste', the 'preservation of standards', and the 'common pursuit of true judgment', involved issues deeper than politics or prior to politics. It was on them that the health of politics, of all social and economic developments, ultimately depended, and not vice versa.

What could have suited me better? There I was, having chosen to sunder myself from South Africa and to settle in England; and here was Dr Leavis, in prose which again and again seemed to reach to the very heart of certain literary works, implicitly proposing an ideal community which could be experienced (if anywhere) only inside my own head, but which nevertheless felt more like the real thing than any other I could imagine myself joining. It was as if the 'Republic of Letters', to use a phrase Leavis would probably have abominated, had been opened up or transformed into a homeland: a place in which I could be naturalised without seeking a licence from any authority other than that of my own tastes or talents, inclinations or ambitions.

But what of the authority of the man who had made all this seem reasonable or plausible? We met only once – well, twice to be exact, at dinner one evening and at breakfast the next morning. By the time of our meeting I had published two or three novels and many short stories, and had been reviewing books fairly regularly in some of the London papers. I was invited by the chairman of the Downing College literary society to give a talk to his group; in the course of his letter he had said that Dr Leavis would be glad to be my host at the high table before the meeting. This was a lure I was quite unable to resist; my curiosity was far stronger than any misgivings I may have felt at the prospect.

We met on the staircase outside Leavis's rooms in the college. I had been brought there by the young man who had written to me. Now he conferred briefly with Leavis about the arrangements, and departed. A moment later we followed, Leavis leading the way, into the court. It was quite dark. At intervals lights shone from windows on to a stone pathway that ran alongside the buildings ranged at stern right angles to one another. The court was so wide, and so open to the sky, the surface of which was just visible by its own light, that all the pre-dinner comings and goings seemed bleak and desultory, rather than cosy. Leavis still walked slightly ahead of me. His gait was rapid, even impatient. We did not have far to go. We passed through another doorway, went up a few more stairs, and plunged into a room crowded with dons ritualistically but eagerly drinking their sherry. By that time I had been overcome by a most unexpected and inappropriate emotion. I felt a kind of protective zeal towards my host.

To protect *him*? From what? From himself, chiefly. He was much frailer than I had expected him to be. He was more tense. Above all, he was more childlike. Each of these qualities seemed to be inseparable from the others. He was childlike because he was so frail, frail because he was so tense, tense because he was as little capable as a child of distancing himself from what he felt about anything or restraining himself from uttering whatever happened to be in his mind. Within a few seconds of our meeting he had told me that he was exhausted – exhausted – and then, touching his chest with his hand and looking at me with a triumphant slyness and earnestness, he said, 'It's lucky for me I have a long-distance runner's heart.' His hand was small, even delicate; it was also as brown and sinewy as everything else about him. The energy of his movements, of his gaze and of the carriage of his head, seemed to have nothing muscular about it; it seemed to be sustained solely by nerve and will and the appetite for combat that went with them. He was dressed in a khaki shirt, a reddish-brown tweed jacket, and a pair of grey flannel trousers. Around his neck, in honour of the formal dinner we were about to attend, was a crumpled tie; the collar button of his shirt, however, was undone. His face was small, brown, narrow-chinned, sharp-nosed, ill-shaven; it was dwarfed by its own brow, from beneath which a pair of almost bird-bright eyes peeped out. Lined and, for all its size, somehow crowded, his brow was not to be distinguished or separated from the scalp to which it was joined. It was the most complicated scalp I had ever seen: flecked, freckled, blotched, mottled, pitted, bumpy, bordered at the back and sides by a fringe of long, fine, unkempt, colourless hair.

On the pathway he told me twice again, without slackening his pace for a moment, how tired he was. On the stairway he told me that his grandfather had supported the Boer cause during the Anglo-Boer War, for which he had been pestered by children in the Cambridge streets, shouting 'Kruger! Kruger!' as he went about his business. Once inside he introduced me to the Master of the college and then carefully instructed me as to what I should do when we were summoned to dinner: I was to fall into place immediately behind the Master and follow him into the hall; he, in turn, would be immediately behind me. A glass of sherry was put into my hand. With an air as energetic and peremptory as before, leaning forward not so much from his hips as from his knees, Leavis asked me if I had seen the editorial in the last issue of the *Times Literary Supplement*. (In those days the *TLS* actually had editorials, odd though it now seems to say so.) I said that I had. He then asked me if I had noticed the reference in it to his 'critical technique'. I said that I had. Leavis smiled like a child who knows and despises the tricks the adults get up to behind his back. 'An insidious word – *technique,*' he said, looking steadily at me. I was impressed by his command of tone and vocabulary, even while I registered how accurate were some of the mimickings of his voice and accent I had heard from former students of his. Then we were interrupted by a young man wearing a clerical collar, who said, a propos of Leavis's standing for election as Professor of Poetry at Oxford, 'I see ——— has thrown her hat into the ring, Dr Leavis!' With no pretence at 'good sportsmanship', and with no regard for the hearty amiability of his interlocutor, Leavis responded instantly and ferociously: 'Yes – an insufferable woman!' The young man's face stiffened; then he broke into a giggle which was instantly quenched in his sherry glass.

There it was: this fiercely unguarded response which affected me, much to my surprise, as if it were a display of some kind of vulnerability. I wanted to draw him aside and tell him that in life, in real life, one doesn't say that sort of thing over a glass of sherry to someone who was evidently not an intimate, in the presence of a complete stranger: least of all does one say it about a person with whom one is in competition for a post. In life, in my life, in the life of everyone else I knew, one guards oneself by guarding one's words; one exposes as little as possible of oneself to repudiation, retribution or (perhaps worst of all) condescension. But not this man, evidently.

Despite his warning I missed my cue when dinner was announced; whereupon Leavis took me urgently by the sleeve so that I might go ahead of him, in due order, as we trooped into the hall. I sat between him and the head of the college, who had one end of the table to himself; across the table from me sat another guest, a high court judge, whose name and face I have forgotten, but whose beautiful grey suit and stiff white collar still stick in the mind. I was seated with my back to the body of the hall and thus saw practically nothing of the students. No sooner had the meal begun than I realised that it was going to be like one in a fairy tale or moral fable. It wasn't that the dishes disappeared every time I reached towards them. They were there for me, all right. It was for my host that they did not exist. With grave courtesy the college servants poured wine for him, put the soup before him, an *entrée*, the main course, the vegetables that accompanied it, the pudding. He touched none of them. Everyone around him, myself included, ate. When we were finished the waiters removed our dishes, pausing each time, with a courtesy as grave as before, for Leavis's assent to the removal of his. I had heard that as a result of injuries sustained during the First World War he was confined to a strict diet; hence his abstinence, presumably, to which neither of us referred. The effect of it, however, was to add to the strain I was under; I felt like some kind of gross creature, sitting there stuffing myself with meat and potatoes, instead of merely watching the comestibles come and go, like my host. From time to time I exchanged civilities with the Master, who at least was in the same boat as myself.

So far from Leavis taking advantage of the circumstances in order to conduct a monologue during the meal, as he has been accused by others of doing on other occasions, I have a clear memory of the attentiveness and encouragement of his manner, of the readiness with which he listened to what I said, of the punctiliousness with which he waited whenever it appeared that I was about to speak. Because of my feeding habits, waiting was sometimes necessary. Not surprisingly I can recall only one topic from that conversation; a topic so predictably 'Leavisian' as to seem almost parodic now. We talked about George Eliot and D. H. Lawrence; more specifically about *Middlemarch* and *Women in Love*. I remember saying that Eliot was more generous to her characters, especially the characters of whom she disapproved, than Lawrence was to his – he exulted over Gerald Crich's downfall, whereas she grieved over Lydgate's. After some consideration of this, Leavis said that he wasn't happy with either of the verbs I had used. He did not suggest others, however.

The meal seemed to go on for a long time. At last the Master rose to his feet and the rest of us got up and began to file out after him. We had taken only a step or two when Leavis threw his head back, and, with a two-handed, choking gesture, tore his tie away from his neck. The meal had gone on for a long time for him too. He had a horror, I had been told, of anything that constricted his neck; that too went back to his experiences in the trenches more than forty years before. Outside the hall I was handed over once again to my undergraduate host. As he left, Leavis told me that he was looking forward to my talk. So was Mrs Leavis. They would join me later.

When I had received the invitation to give a talk, and had seen that Leavis would be my host at dinner, it had occurred to me as a possibility, though not as a likely one, that he might choose to come to the meeting. Partly for this reason, and partly because I had had little to do with the academic world or with academic occasions of any kind since I had been a student at the university in Johannesburg, I had taken a great deal of trouble over what I was going to say. In fact, I had written out every word of it, as if it were a lecture to be given on some formal occasion, not a talk to an undergraduate society. Now, as I made conversation with some of the students who were gathering to hear me, and with a tall, melancholy, prematurely bald young man, in a grey overcoat, who was evidently Leavis's assistant in the teaching of English within the College, I congratulated myself on my forethought. Everything I had to say was there, waiting for me, in the breast pocket of my jacket.

I congratulated myself doubly when the meeting began, with Dr and Mrs Leavis sitting side by side directly in front of me, dominating an audience that couldn't have consisted of more than about a dozen other people. Because of my anxieties the piece I had written was solemnly academic in manner and gloomy in content. Whatever its faults, it was all there, anyway, and I proceeded to read it. Page One was negotiated without mishap; Page Two likewise; Three, Four, Five ditto. With the confidence of habit I turned to Page Six, only to find myself staring at Page Seven. Page Six wasn't there. I had left it at home. The shock was all the greater because I had been depending wholly on the typescript throughout: I felt exactly (the inevitable analogy) like a man at the foot of a staircase who takes a step that isn't there. For a long time, or what seemed to be a long time, I was silent; then, hobbling a bit, groping a bit, stammering a bit, staring quite a lot at the modest moulding where the ceiling met the far wall of the room, I finally made it to Page Seven. From then on all I had to do was to slog through to the end. Which I did.

Only to discover that it wasn't the end. Question time had begun. Mrs Leavis wasted no time. In the course of my talk I had tried to present an anatomy of the 'colonial' literary situation: inevitably, the way it had come out was as a catalogue of lacks and deficiencies. The sum of her questioning amounted to her asking me what I proposed doing about those lacks and deficiencies. There was no point in my coming to Cambridge to talk to *them* on the subject. Why didn't I go back to South Africa and talk about it there, or emigrate to New Zealand and talk to the New Zealanders about it? Or was I merely pretending to be concerned about the problem? Wearing a black cardigan of almost institutional severity, she kept her circular face and circular glasses trained firmly on me. This *ad hominem* grilling went on for some time. It went on, in fact, until Leavis roused himself to say, in a whisper which he made no attempt to render inaudible, 'You can't ask a man those sorts of questions!' So, as things had turned out, he was the one protecting me. He did it pretty effectively too. Mrs Leavis fell silent. Some of the students present, one of them also from South Africa, joined in the discussion, which went on in desultory fashion for a few minutes. I was thanked by the chairman for my talk, and a polite round of applause followed.

We went to another room for coffee. Now that the public part of the proceedings was over, Mrs Leavis relented, and came over and conversed quite amiably with me. Evidently she did not bear me a grudge either for the punishment she had inflicted on me or for the rebuke her husband had administered. When the Leavises got up to go I said goodbye to them and thanked him for taking me to the dinner. Everyone relaxed after they had gone, even the tutor. He and I talked about common acquaintances: a conversation I cannot now recall without recalling also that more than two decades later I was to read in a newspaper that that uneasy, faintly smiling, shiny-headed man, whom I was never to see again, had been battered to death by an unknown assailant.

Then the evening was over, really over, at last. I retired to the guest bedroom provided for me. Getting into bed I nearly broke my toe on a completely cold hot-water-bottle, made of glazed stoneware. It was an item of a kind I had seen previously only in the windows of junk shops.

Next morning a steward showed me into the combination room for breakfast. It was a large room, of which I remember little but various shades and planes of highly polished, dark wood. And chairs. On one of those planes of wood a single place had been laid for breakfast. In solitude and silence I began to eat my corn flakes. To one side of the room were glass doors looking out on a quiet garden. I seem to remember, perhaps erroneously, that it was through those doors, and not through the door I had used, that Leavis came in. He had obviously wanted to see me again; indeed he said so. He had come to the college because he had a letter to write and wanted to compose it in peace; but he had hoped that he might still find me there. I was surprised and gratified by this attention. My only regret was that once again I had been caught with my mouth full.

His manner, as he sat down across the table from me, was relaxed, compared at least with how I had found it the previous evening. Yet I had the impression once again of instantly finding myself in the vicinity of a ceaseless, relentless mental and emotional activity, sustained wholly from within, which manifested itself as much in the posture of his body as in the cadences of his voice, as much in the choice of subjects to talk about as in some of the motives and states of mind his language made transparent. The letter he had come to write, he told me, was a delicate one. He was on the point of retiring. To mark the occasion the college had commissioned a portrait to be hung in the hall or elsewhere. However, a problem had arisen. He and his wife had seen some of the work of the man who had been approached to do the job, and had not cared for it. 'He's a man who goes around the country painting portraits of distinguished people – without any distinction at all.' But how to indicate that he, the subject, the sitter, the recipient of the honour, was not happy with the choice made by the college and wanted another man to carry out the task? His wife could not see that there was any difficulty. According to her, all he had to do was to tell them that he wouldn't have their man. She didn't understand, he said, that in dealing with such a topic there came a time when one couldn't accept anyone else's suggestions – 'no matter *who* they come from or *how* forcefully they are put . . .'

Later he told me that as a young man he had been urged to take the newly established chair of English at the university I had attended in Johannesburg. 'They' had told him it would be a wonderful opportunity for him – a new chair, a new university, a new country. 'They wanted to get rid of me,' he said, as if it were the most obvious remark in the world for him to have made at that juncture; one so obvious as to need neither any special emphasis nor anything further by way of explanation. Yet in his voice, for all the off-handedness with which he had just spoken, there was something of the child's guile and triumph in outwitting the adults' stupid schemings; and, as well, the closely hugged desolation of a lifetime's anger and misery.

Not until many years had passed, incidentally, did it occur to me that that remark of his ('They wanted to get rid of me') threw an unexpected light on the exchanges about 'colonial' culture between his wife and myself, the previous evening, and on the way in which he had eventually brought them to an end.

It would be wrong, though, for me to give the impression that he was the only one who talked over that breakfast table. The conversation rambled rather: from 'those subaltern books', as he called them, about the First World War (Graves, Sassoon, Blunden etc.) to the drinking habits of a well-known reviewer of the day, since deceased. Throughout he was as courteous and considerate towards me as he could possibly have been. He insisted on walking across the college court with me, to see me back to the room where I had left my overnight bag. As we made our way across the quadrangle, now gleaming mildly in the morning sunlight, he pointed out a space to one side where they were building, or had recently built, what he described with a sudden access of venom as '*dentists' houses*'. We shook hands and he turned smartly and went back the way he had come, walking even more rapidly, now that he was on his own, than before. In the years that followed I dreamed about him, improbably and affectionately, several times. And I kept up, though with an ever-increasing sense of distance and scepticism, with the essays he went on publishing almost to the very end.

THE
—————— VANISHING ACT ——————

We expect our children's childhood to pass as slowly as we remember our own to have done. And so it does – *to them*. To them a week or a month or a year can appear ocean-like in its expanses of sameness or changeableness. To us, however, to the parents we have become, the childhood of our children passes as swiftly as everything else in adult years. From moment to moment, we feel, we are left vainly grasping after people who are no longer there. They have vanished even while we were looking at them. How can we recall the six-week-old infant when he has been shouldered out of his own life and out of our minds by someone of the same name and with something of the same features who is now six months old; and how can we recall the six-month-old infant when another infant aged two years or three years or five years has taken his place? And the fifteen-year-old who replaces that five-year-old will in turn be swiftly replaced by an adult with whom our relationship is bound to be quite different from the other, provisional relationships we had before with all his or her other, provisional selves.

True, we change as adults too; we change more rapidly than we are willing to acknowledge, whether in looking at ourselves or others. But the speed and extent of those changes cannot be compared with the metamorphoses our children pass through. Where have they gone, those earlier avatars of their selfhood, those forms they assumed for this moment or that? Into photograph albums, it seems, and anecdote; if anywhere. ('Do you remember that time . . .?' 'Well, when she was about three she used to . . .') But photographs and anecdotes are a poor exchange for living recollections, recollections of figures so full of life they seem substantial enough to blot out the light behind them. Other loves, other acquaintances, people older than ourselves or contemporary with ourselves, we can remember in that fashion, even after a lapse of years, even when such people may have meant little to us. Of our children, of our children's younger selves, virtually nothing remains. When we try to think of them as they once were (perhaps a few months ago!) we have to be content, all too often, with unexpected, unanchored fragments. A forgotten item of clothing seen by chance in a drawer, for example, will perhaps produce not so much a visual image as some sort of tactile reawakening within the self, a 'feel' of having handled the small body which the garment once covered. Revisiting, on our own, a place we have been to with our children, we may find them suddenly revisiting us: not as individuals who were then of this height or whose hair was cut in that way, but as urgent *presences* merely, beings whose hands were in our own or slipping away from them, whose voices were raised or silent. What those presences also bring back is not so much a recollection of our emotions as of theirs: their eagerness, their curiosity, their anxiety, their readiness to run ahead or to retreat, their imperious hungers or uncurtailable rages, their collapses into sleepiness or indifference. Only in that context can we recall the sensation, private to us, unknown to them, of having been in charge, of having been under pressure, of having once been parents.

That is all. We can hardly blame ourselves for feeling that it isn't enough. The children have gone and have taken with them the emotions they aroused, as if into an abyss deeper than that into which every other passion from the past eventually falls. Passions of sexual love, or of fear, or of ambition, or of the shame or pride we felt as children in the parents we once had – those in some sense are still with us; they remain accessible in the memory, attached to particular scenes or experiences. But the physical and moral passions of parenthood, which any parent knows to be as deep, as startling, as much a remaking of the whole self as any other, turn out also to be as evanescent as the constantly self-transforming bodies which had aroused them. Protectiveness and wonder; a sense of being nakedly needed and of needing to be needed; infatuations with shades and textures of skin and hair, with knees and fingernails, with flawless eyes and hollow napes of necks, with lips moister and more delicate than any others we have kissed; pleasures of touching, stroking, smelling, gazing, encompassing; fatigues, irritations, bewilderments, clenched anxieties over illnesses and unexplained absences; incredulity at the responsibilities we have assumed and the half-ashamed delight in finding our way back to much of what we had lost from the time of our own infancy – all once there, and all gone. Gone, leaving so few particular, individual, moment-attached tracings or scorings in the mind.

No wonder, then, that there should be so many works of literature which deal with family relationships from the child's point of view and so few which deal with those relationships from that of the parent. The absence of literature on the subject – I am not speaking of child-rearing manuals – is in fact one of the reasons why succeeding generations of parents are so surprised at what they find themselves going through. No one has warned them! Like the rest of us, writers can recall, sometimes all too clearly or fondly, what it was like to be a child. But to know what it is to be a parent, or to recall what it was to have been a parent, is a much more elusive and problematical business. Think of all those books about children and their parents, or parent-figures, to be found among the literary classics (and think of the movies, or of the novels with other names, which are derived at a greater or lesser remove from them) – *The Mill on the Floss* and *David Copperfield*, *Mansfield Park* and *Jane Eyre*, *Tom Jones* and *War and Peace*, *Sons and Lovers* and *Portrait of the Artist as a Young Man*. All are in effect novels about being a child and having a parent or parents, and about growing out of them, not about being a parent and having a child and having it grow out of you. So are plays like *The Oresteia* or *Romeo and Juliet* or *Hamlet*. (How much we are given of Hamlet's feelings about his mother and stepfather; what ugly, truncated glimpses we are given of their feelings about him.) And so one could go on, almost indefinitely. *The Metamorphosis*, *Swann's Way*, *Great Expectations*, *The Brothers Karamazov*, *The Tin Drum* . . . And on the other side? One has to struggle to think of them. *Silas Marner*, *Dombey and Son* perhaps, Turgenev's *Fathers and Sons*, and indubitably the greatest of all such works, and great partly because it adopts with such passion the parental point of view, *King Lear*. (Think how easy it would have been to present sympathetically, from their perspective, the problems of the two daughters, Goneril and Regan, confronted as they are with an aged father who has nothing to do with his time and energy but disrupt their domestic arrangements. If only either woman had had a 'granny flat' in her castle!) The Bible, interestingly enough, also gives us more of King David's dealings with his errant sons from David's point of view than from theirs; he is the one who really matters, whose hurts and hopes really count; not they and theirs. And that's about all.

None of this (which we take so much for granted that I have never seen it remarked on elsewhere) is accidental. The drama of parenthood from within – and the loss of it, which is part of its drama – remains the great unexplored subject of imaginative writing; in comparison with it, supposedly taxing subjects like the end of the world or the inner life of a mad dictator can appear positively banal. The trouble is, though, that the subject is unexplored because it is largely unexplorable. The emotions of parenthood are experienced in a way and at a level distinctive to themselves, and then they vanish, along with the children who occasion them, to whom they are devoted, and who never rest from carrying out their task of transforming themselves, moment by moment, into other beings.

Until at last they succeed to such an extent that they cease to be children. 'Have you any children?' a well-known Scottish poet was once asked. 'No,' he replied, in grimly humorous, Scottish fashion, 'I have a man and a woman.' It goes without saying that his relationship with 'his' man and woman, and theirs with him, will be forever affected by the fact that they were once his children; in some respects which will be obvious to both sides, and in others which will be hidden from them, they will continue to respond to one another according to patterns laid down in their earliest years together. But what will also become increasingly obvious to both sides is that the balance of responsibility and dependence between them has begun to swing slowly but inexorably in the other direction.

Just as the parents of young children feel bound to protect and help them, to shield them from the ugliness of life and its dangers, so grown children begin to feel that they have this obligation towards their parents. When they keep silent about events or emotions in their own lives, it is not because they are afraid of their parents' anger or disapproval, as before, but because they are indifferent to them, or because their parents have begun to acquire in their eyes something of the innocence of children, the pathos of their ignorance; like children they seem to have become especially vulnerable to mental and physical injury. And indeed, if parents live long enough, and suffer the illnesses and deprivations which age inevitably brings, they will revert to being children, wrinkled children, impossible children; beings whom their children will care for out of affection, out of pity, out of piety, out of exasperation, out of regard for the past; hardly out of passion.

Well, one can see the sense of it, if it is not our wills or individual circumstances but the continuation of the race which ultimately determines such matters. Children are lovable, and are loved, precisely because and to the degree that they are vulnerable. Their vulnerability is signalled in every possible fashion: in their stature, in the shape of their heads, their halting speech, the softness of their skins, their eager movements. If we were not moved to cherish them by such manifestations of weakness, the race would not survive. The vulnerability of old people, on the other hand, has no such appeal; they have exhausted their usefulness, racially speaking, and nature has no compunction in making this fact as evident to everyone around them as it makes the charm and vitality of children. However, only megalomaniacs are given to thinking of themselves as representatives of the race or of nature. The rest of us, parents of children and children of parents, are kept busy enough trying to cope, as best we can, with all the vicissitudes of role, with all the plaitings together and unravellings of relationships, which are forced in such remorseless succession and simultaneity upon us.

Now, an anecdote. A story of the kind which Coleridge, in 'The Nightingale', describing how he held up his infant to the moon, so that the tears in the baby's eyes glittered in the moonlight, calls 'a father's tale'. In other words, an episode treasured not because of its weight but precisely because of its smallness or fragility, its transience, its everydayness – these being the very qualities out of which and into which the intense emotions of parenthood grow. The child who appears in the tale, and who has since been transformed into a young man driving around London in a battered yellow van, selling 'whole foods' from door to door, has of course no recollection of the incident. But then, I am pretty sure that if I had not made a note of it at the time, it would have slipped out of my memory like innumerable other incidents or perceptions, some no doubt even smaller, some which must have seemed more weighty, which in their turn clutched quite as fiercely at my heart. The occasions of feeling once lost, all that remains is the conviction that the feeling was once there.

Soon after my son's third birthday a departing neighbour foisted a pet budgerigar on our household. *Faute de mieux* we accepted it, and hung up the cage in the hall. The bird was male; it was canary-yellow all over, except for its head and neck which were stippled blue. Sometimes, when it stretched out a wing, a wave of iridiscent light, which was neither blue nor yellow, or was both at once, would pass from its neck along its wing. Then it would stretch out a leg, too, sideways under the wing, as if to hold it up, like the spar of an umbrella. Having completed the movement, it would regain its balance before solemnly repeating the step on the other side, in ballet-dancer fashion. Its eyes were bright and never gave anything away; its beak was tiny and so fiercely bent over itself you couldn't help feeling its breath must have been as stertorous as an old man's, if only your ears had been sharp enough to hear it. It never sang or chirped much, this budgie, and talked not at all, but it climbed up and down its toy ladder, and gazed with cocked head at itself in the little, plastic-backed looking-glass that was suspended in the corner of the cage; occasionally it swung itself back and forth on a kind of trapeze provided for it, and bit languidly at the bars which kept it imprisoned. It ate in little flurries, and drank with a haughty, connoisseur-like deliberation at the water in its bowl.

That was when it was well. Some weeks after we had taken charge of it, however, it fell ill. One day it moped, the next day its feathers no longer lay smoothly over and under each other; on the morning of the third day my son called me urgently to come to the cage to see what had happened. The bird lay in a queerly uncomfortable position; one that no living creature would have been able to sustain. Its shoulders were hunched up, its beak rested on the floor of the cage and was turned to one side, its tail pointed upwards. The rest of it was nothing: some feathers one could blow away with a breath, a foot like a barbed grass-seed. Death had not had to make much of an effort to carry it off.

It was hard to say, though, what it was about the bird that had so roused my son's misgiving. Its immobility? Its hunched posture? The fact that it lay on the floor of the cage? An instinctive alarm aroused by all of these? Anyway, just as the condition of the bird had somehow spoken to him of death, so everything about him, as he stood beneath the cage, looking up at it, spoke to me of life: his stillness as much as his movement, his silence as much as his speech, the light that came off him and the light that seemed to be within him. His hair gleamed, his eyes flashed green, his skin was suffused with its own glow; there were stars, white stars and dark stars, in his open mouth. I could hardly bear it, somehow that his eyelids were paler than the skin around them. He was wearing a green knitted jersey with a stand-up collar and buttons at its neck, and a pair of orange pants of a coarsely woven material that seemed to come no more than about two inches down his thighs.

'The bird's dead,' I told him.

The word itself seemed to mean little to him. 'What does he do when he's dead?'

'Nothing. We must bury it.'

'Berry? What means *berry*?'

'We put it in the ground.'

'Why?'

'Because it's dead.'

'Are you going to do it now?'

'Yes.'

'Can I watch?'

'Yes.'

I took the cage off its hook and went with it to the garden at the back of the house. The day was pale, the sky was high, the air cold: one of those days in early spring when it is hard to believe that the sunlight will ever have enough warmth to start the whole business of the year afresh. I picked up a trowel and the two of us knelt at the edge of a flower bed. When I opened the door of the cage and tried to get at the bird with my fingers, I found that the aperture was too small; my fingers could hardly get in. So, holding up the cage, I removed the sliding tray beneath it which made up its floor. The bird fell stiffly, straight downwards, its tiny length revolving vertically once in the air before it hit the ground. As it fell my son cried out in amazement, with an unmistakeable note of pity and fear in his voice, 'Ah, the budgie's *all* dead!'

It took me only a moment to dig a hole and flick the bird into it. This produced a cry of dismay: 'Don't do that! You'll hurt the budgie!' It was already almost out of sight. Only a few feathers were showing. Another trowelful and they were gone. I tamped down the earth and got to my feet. My son had risen first. His body was framed by the matted, pallid oblong of lawn behind him. From below he fixed on me a look of outrage and disbelief.

'How's the budgie going to get out now?' he demanded.

'It doesn't want to get out,' I replied. The inappropriateness of the phrase was apparent to me the moment it was out of my mouth. Wanting? Not wanting? That stiff, befeathered morsel, crushed beneath some lumps of earth? We were the one who had wants: he to protect the bird from its death; I to protect him from his; both of us to do what we could not.

FROM GENERATION
————————— TO GENERATION —————————

On my desk, as I write, is a book of an unfashionable and awkward size. Fourteen inches long and eight inches wide, it has the shape of a somewhat enlarged sheet of foolscap. It is cheaply produced. The paper is coarse, fragile, and pale brown in colour rather than white; the covers are made not of cloth but of greyish, absorbent cardboard; the spine is covered by a strip of black material which has come away for much of its length; the pages have evidently been sewn together either by hand or by some extremely primitive machine.

For reasons which will be explained later, I can read only the introduction of this book. I know that it was put together from the posthumous writings of my great-grandfather and distributed by one of my great-uncles. The person who gave it to me told me that it is of no interest and of no merit whatever. The introduction, on the other hand, says that the book was compiled so that the memory of the author's 'loftiness of spirit' might be passed 'from generation to generation'. Since I am unable to read it, all I can pass on is a description of how the book came into my possession, and what happened to both the person who gave it to me and the man responsible for producing it.

The story told below is, in other words, a domestic one, a piece of family history. It deals with madness, inconsolable loss, the movement of people across continents, and the murder of those left behind; as well as with our instinctive belief that order and continuity truly express the nature of our lives, and that everything which is not orderly and continuous is a mistake, a perversion of what has been, should be, and will be.

Family histories have no real beginnings or ends. I may as well begin in the middle, then, with a telephone call to my home in London, which summoned me to a Hampstead hospital about a mile away. An uncle of mine had given my name to one of the ward sisters and had asked her to phone me. She told me that he had been brought in a few days previously, after a fall. He had been in a confused state. And now? He was a good deal better.

That was not how my uncle saw his condition. He had just one word to describe what he was going through. It was a word he had just invented, though he was obviously unaware of having done so.

'Tormentation!'

He said it loudly several times, with long intervals between each exclamation. He had managed to lift his head off the pillow by hanging on to the tightly tucked-in sheets and blankets that came half-way up his chest; he had used them like ropes to haul himself up. Now he let go, and his head sank back. But his eyes, filled with despair and self-pity, remained fixed on mine.

The ward was underground; his bed was the one nearest the door. Just a few feet away was a kind of landing or vestibule, through which I had come, with a flight of stairs and a lift-shaft of metal grilles and angle-iron going up from it. The lift itself was like an ancient, upended tram-car; it was constantly ascending and descending, with a whine and a hiss and a clashing of its doors. Needless to say, its noise was one source of the tormentation my uncle was going through.

Looking around, I could see others. Because the ward was sub-terranean, it had no windows at all. Whatever daylight there was entered from above, by way of thick glass slabs let into the ceiling. Through them, if you tried hard enough, you could just discern the wavering outlines of the walls of the courtyard above. The patients were trapped like fish under ice, able only to stare upwards at what was imprisoning them. Moreover, the ward was not only underground but also circular in shape. Its hub was a plastered column of immense girth; its rim, the outer wall; its spokes, the beds ranged in two rings, with a space between them. Everything was thus set out in concentric bands: wall, beds, passageway, beds, hub. If you turned your head too quickly they all revolved with you. No doubt they did it even more readily if you were wounded, or had a fever, or had taken a variety of drugs, or had had some part of your body excised, or had lain there for a few days listening to the groans of others in a worse plight than your own.

And then there were the nurses. Or so my uncle claimed. The sight of one of them passing his bed – a fresh, harmless-looking girl – suddenly produced whole sentences from him. 'These women here,' he said, 'are merciless. They're like demons. All of them. They haven't one shred, not one scrap, of human feeling. No sweetness.'

He frowned; he pursed his lips; he reached forward with his eyes and face, so to speak, without moving his head. It was an expression which belonged wholly to my mother: I saw her, not him, when he made it. 'Never a smile,' he said. All the creases on his face deepened and ran into one another, and he began to cry. His sobs were like sneezes: abrupt, spasmodic, each one coming after an interval of silence. He wiped his eyes and nose with his fingers; then reached for a handkerchief under his pillow and did the job again. Before falling silent he brought out the most formal sentence I had yet heard from him. 'Their cruelty is indescribable.'

He lay on his back, no longer looking at me. His eyelids fluttered a few times; presently they came down and stayed down, and he appeared at once to fall asleep. His full, strong, square mouth was closed; it was the one part of his face which still seemed to know its own purpose, to be in possession of itself. For the rest I saw only meat-coloured abrasions, gauze dressings, sunken cheeks, wide, vulnerable nostrils that flickered or twitched irregularly, a grey-blue stubble of beard. He was wearing a striped, hospital-issue pyjama jacket; the top button was undone, revealing an almost foam-like growth of grizzled hair that came right up to the neck-line. To the side of his bed was a steel cabinet; unlike the others in the ward, its top was pathetically bare. There were no books on it, no magazines, no flowers, no delicacies in tins or boxes; only a carafe of water, a drinking glass, and his spectacles neatly squatting, with folded shafts and lenses tilted upwards, on the shiny surface.

The next bed was occupied by another old man, older than my uncle by perhaps ten or fifteen years. He also lay on his back with his eyes closed. One of his hands was held in the fierce clasp of a woman only a little less grey and shrivelled than himself, who was sitting on a chair to the side of the bed; while he slept she studied his face with such absorption, with an expression of such tender-ness, it looked almost wanton or abandoned. Beyond them was a young man both of whose arms, clad in plaster casts to above the elbows, were motionlessly thrust out before him; on the cabinet beside his bed, in pride of place, was a red motor cycle helmet with various legends painted in white on it: 'Zap!' 'Go man go!' and so forth. Presumably he had injured himself in a crash on his bike, and the helmet was put there like a totem or fetish, to show the world that he was still what he had been before the smash, and worshipped where he had worshipped before. There were various other pyjamaed and dressing-gowned men sitting and talking to their wives; there was another youngster who was fixedly reading a thick text-book from a pile of books on the cabinet next to his bed; there was a bed wholly screened-off by dark green curtains, through which no one passed and from which no sound came.

And so on, as far as my eye could make it around the hub, and then back to my uncle. Since he showed no sign of waking, I decided to go in search of the ward sister, to learn from her as much as I could about the circumstances which had led to his admission. I found her in a little office on the landing, under the stairs. She was a thickset, small-faced woman of middle age, almost rubbery in appearance somehow, though not at all in the sense of being pliant; rather, she was resistant, not easy to get at, strictly a non-conductor of emotions and responses. She wore the faintly striped dress and full-length, starched white apron, with a watch and various badges of rank pinned to it, which was the uniform of the place; her hair was pulled tight into the elaborate cap she wore, an item as stiff and formal in shape as an architectural feature on top of a column. She was not, I learned, the sister who had phoned me; in fact, before divulging any information about my uncle she demanded that I explain my relationship to him and how I came to be visiting him. When I had answered her questions satisfactorily she proceeded to tell me what she knew – which was not all that much more than I had already heard. Apparently he had slipped and fallen in the street, and had struck his head on the pavement; so far as was known no vehicle or cyclist had been involved in the accident; some anonymous person (from a shop, she thought) had phoned for an ambulance. One could imagine the scene: the old man on the pavement, the passers-by, the stoppers and starers, the helping hand eventually extended, the small drama of the ambulance's arrival and departure. That had been five days before. He had been concussed on his arrival, but not very seriously. That wasn't the problem. Not the real problem.

She regarded me steadily; then, convinced that her dark grey eyes and thick brows had done their job of intimidation, she surprised me by lapsing into euphemism; indeed, the language of the nursery. 'He's been very naughty,' she said. 'He's been taking a lot of stuff that hasn't been very good for him.'

A silence followed. I had nothing to say to what I had just heard. In response to my asking her when she thought he would be discharged from the hospital, she said that he might be ready to go in a week or ten days. They wouldn't want him to leave any sooner. And then? Well, they had got his address from the diary that had been found in his pocket, and had phoned his landlady to tell her what had happened. She had said that he had paid the rent for his room until the end of the month, so there wasn't anything to worry about as far as that was concerned. He'd be able to go back there when he left the hospital. But they were anxious that he should have 'calmed down' by then.

From what I had seen of him there seemed little chance of this happening while he remained there. But I did not say this; instead I asked if he could be moved to another ward, or perhaps just to a bed farther from the door. The sister said that she would see what she could do; but the voice in which she said these words, and the unblinking, unyielding stare which accompanied them, told me that she could do what she liked, and that that was exactly what she was going to do. Never, but never, anything else.

My uncle, who had been very naughty, who had been taking a lot of stuff that wasn't good for him, was still asleep on his back when I returned to the ward. His mouth seemed to have tightened as he slept; deep lines, like those on the jaw of a ventriloquist's dummy, now ran straight down from the corners of his lips into his chin. I left him lying like that: as if he were waiting to be given more words to say.

My uncle the addict . . . My mother's oldest brother, the narco-maniac . . . The rabbi's oldest son, the junkie . . . .

As a novelist I might be tempted to repudiate what I have just written. As an autobiographer I cannot do so. I have no choice. It happened. It was so. Out there in South Africa, in the bare, colonial provinces, he had virtually invented addiction for himself. Or on his own terms, at least. He was not a young man when he became an addict; he was old, in his early fifties, as old as the century itself had been at that date. He wasn't in the fashion then; he had pre-ceded it. He wasn't the black sheep of the family: on the contrary, he was its most adored, most admired figure, the oldest brother of a flock of sisters who bowed their heads to him, a conscientious husband, the father of two promising children. And if, in relation to his condition, such ironies were not crude enough, there was yet another, perhaps cruder still. For many years his profes-sion had been that of social worker; he had been a paid adviser to people who were incapable of managing their lives for themselves. Put that in a novel! Part psychiatrist, part employment officer, part teacher, part father and uncle to mankind in general, he had cultivated the manner appropriate to these roles: stern but compassionate, attentive yet already weary of what he was about to hear, pompous and yet conscientiously aware of his own frailty, too.

That was how I had left him in Johannesburg, when I set out for Europe; the continent from which he and his sisters had come a generation and more previously. Then I began to hear vague talk from visiting relations and acquaintances of his having had a 'nervous breakdown', and of 'spells' he had had in mental hospitals. His wife had left him. His job was in danger. At last one of the visitors said, 'Don't you know? Do you really not know? He's a drug addict.' He had originally become addicted to pethedine, apparently, which had been given to him during a sciatic attack; but he would now take absolutely anything if he had to: tranquillisers, pep pills, codeine, morphine mixtures, cough linctus, aspirin.

What all these had done to him I saw for the first time when I flew back to South Africa to attend my mother's funeral. His glasses low on his nose; his eyes cast eternally down, with a thick light in them or on them; his hat set far back on his head, like that of a jaunty punter at the races; his feet moving in a random manner, as if at every step they expected to find the ground an inch or two higher than it actually was; his mouth pursed forward and opening every now and again, as he smacked his lips and uncomfortably pushed his tongue against the back of his lower teeth; his fingers fumbling continually in the shallow pockets of his waistcoat; a look of blank incomprehension on his face, together with an agonizingly slow, sunken determination to be left out of nothing: it was in this shape that he arrived in Kimberley by plane from Johannesburg. It was in this shape that he followed the coffin of his sister, who had so much admired his sagacity and benignity; that he poured on to the coffin the obligatory shovelful of dry Kimberley sand; that he sat through the lunch at the house, after the funeral, with the other members of the family; that he went out for a walk with me, once the lunch was over.

He took the walk slowly. He had to. We went along an unpaved road near the house. When I had been a child the veld had begun where we walked: tufts of grass, thorn trees, ant-heaps, rock out-crop, red earth, in disorderly sequence and inconsequence, stretch-ing away forever. Now there were new houses to the side of the road, each one with a wire fence and the beginnings of a garden before it; on the other side was an embankment of earth and some playing fields. Our footsteps crunched on the sand. My uncle's hat had come forward over his eyes; his glasses were so low they were in constant danger of falling. My mother was in her grave, under just such hot, dry sand as we were walking on. I remembered our arrival in Kimberley, for the very first time, almost thirty years before: she had passed me through the open window of the railway carriage to my father, who was waiting on the platform below. I had been four years old. It was all over.

My uncle staggered and sighed. He was sunken so deep in his narcotic stupor it was quite impossible to tell if he really knew what the occasion was of his being there, or the significance of the hand-ful of loose earth he had let fall on the echoing wooden box below. Yet the noises he made were those of grief: or if not of grief, then of unhappiness. In some corner of whatever consciousness was left to him he knew that he was in disgrace; he had betrayed the trust his sister had had in him, and had failed a solemn, sorrowful occasion. White stuff collected in the corners of his mouth and remained there, for all the constant movements of his lips. As if under some grotesque disguise I could see in him my mother's vivid brown eye, lighter than his own, and her brow. We said nothing to one another. Once or twice we stopped and stared around. The sun hung motionlessly in a bald sky. Then we went back to the house. His sisters tried to straighten his clothes and shoved his glasses back on his nose; then they put him on the afternoon plane and flew back to Johannesburg with him.

Six years after that funeral he was living alone in London. As I have already said, it was his second migration. In his youth he had gone from Lithuania to South Africa; now, as an old man, he had moved from South Africa to England. During the first migration he had had to act as 'the man of the family', for his mother had recently been widowed and he was the oldest son among a large contingent or consignment of children; almost half a century later he was the dependent, the child, the one in need of care. Jobless, wifeless, homeless, he had followed his grown-up children, who had come to England to advance their academic careers. But as luck would have it (and the timing was just bad luck, as they showed by the care they took of him subsequently) both the children and their spouses departed within a few months of his arrival on one-year fellowships to the United States: one to Princeton, one to UCLA. There my uncle would not or could not follow them. He settled down in London to await their return. With the help of his son, who saw to these matters before his departure, he found a room near the Finchley Road Underground Station; he was put on the list of a general practitioner in the neighbourhood; he was enrolled in a couple of evening classes; for the rest he was left to fill his time as best he could. The charity for which he had worked in Johannesburg, and which had put up with him after his disintegration for far longer than any commercial firm would have done, provided him with a pension that was small but sufficient for his needs.

At first I used to see him pretty regularly. He would come for lunch with my wife and myself about once a fortnight, or perhaps a little more often. He was always early and always apologetic for being early. He wore a blue or brown suit, a relic from his days as a professional man, and brown shoes which he kept in a high state of shininess; around his neck hung a brave if ill-knotted tie. He was obviously making an effort to keep himself together. I knew there were a few other houses, those of other members of the family, and of friends, to whom he made visits similar to the ones he paid to ourselves; he also went into town sometimes to meet visitors from South Africa who had let him know that they were coming.

What else? Well, he went to libraries and read the papers, like many other pensioners. He listened to the radio. (He never acquired the television habit, apparently.) Mostly, he walked about. He told me this and I could see it for myself, for he always arrived and left on foot. Even when it was raining he would not take a bus or a train. Instead he would wait out the worst of the downpour, swathe himself in a voluminous plastic mac with a hood, and march haltingly but with much determination into the aftermath. Sometimes I walked part of the way with him; sometimes I stood at a window and watched him go: relieved that he was going; guilty for not having pressed him to stay longer or come again sooner; incredulous, above all, at what was most incontrovertibly the truth about both of us – that he was he, and I was I. When I had come to Johannesburg, the big city, at the age of seventeen, and was living in digs, his had been one of the houses I could go to for a meal and conversation; I had borrowed books and money from him from time to time, and had occasionally gone for a ride in his little French car with him, his wife, and their two grave children. And before then, long before I had reached that stage, he had been one of the largest of the fixed stars in the family firmament: itself something as mysterious and as much to be taken for granted as the light and darkness of the real sky which hung above me. And now . . .

He was a difficult guest. This was true even during the first few months of the period I am writing about, when he was trying hard to manage, to keep himself going. On the one hand he had his *idées fixes* on a number of subjects: among them, the contemptible nature of all religions, and of the Jewish religion in particular; the incomprehensibility of grown-up men reading (let alone writing!) novels; the state of intellectual darkness, not to say childishness, in which mankind had lived before the important discoveries of Freud about human growth and motivation; the automatic superiority of all things British, and especially of things upper-class British, over all others; and so forth. On the other hand he had his sighs and groans, which would go on for minutes on end: shattering sighs and wholehearted groans, in alternation with vacant stares ahead of him. Then something would distract him (the food put in front of him, or the entrance of one of my children) and he would launch himself again on one of his hobby-horses. Actually, he believed them to be battle-chargers: he knew that my own views on most of these subjects, if not all of them, were different from his own, and he never advanced an argument without hoping it would provoke me in some way. Not provoke me to counter-argument, really; just so long as it provoked me. I could see this in his eye. Behind his glasses, within the strange indeterminacy between pupil and iris which was one of the consequences of his addiction, there lurked something obstinate and perverse; something not to be budged; something which looked at me with a dull gleam of triumph. Or indifference: that too being a triumph of a kind. He'd shown everyone a thing or two: his wife and children, his father the orthodox rabbi, his widowed mother, his admiring sisters who had taken their bearings from him, and had devotedly adopted all his intellectual attitudes. They had followed him into secularism, into a contempt for the East European past and everything that smacked of it, into a veneration for saints of the twentieth century Enlightenment like Bertrand Russell, Bernard Shaw, Havelock Ellis, Sigmund Freud (of course), A. S. Neill, J. B. S. Haldane, and others whose books had been on his shelves at home in Johannesburg. That is, when he had had a home. But who can tell about such matters? For all one knows he may even have felt that he had shown those saints a thing or two, as well.

Not that the sighs and groans weren't also wholly sincere. The price he had paid for this triumph was a terrible one, and he knew it. Once, for no reason that I can recall, he brought a couple of photographs to show me: one taken just before the departure of the family from Lithuania, and another taken just after their arrival in South Africa. In the first the entire group is gathered on the elaborate verandah of a wooden house; in the other they stand in the back yard of a cousin's house in Johannesburg, with washing-line and corrugated iron fence much in evidence; in both of them my uncle is given a position in the centre of the picture, as befits the new head of the family. He wears a serious suit, with many buttons and with small lapels shaped like dog-ears on a book, and he has a serious look on his face. His hair is far thicker and blacker than it was to be decades later, but it starts growing in exactly the same place from the same bays above his forehead, and is compelled to go in exactly the same direction, straight back. Standing over me, unable to bear the pain of looking at the pictures, and unable to look away from them, my uncle said only, 'Ach! Ach!' over and over again.

He had never really spoken to me about life in the old country. All my questions about it had been turned aside with some generalised expression of distaste for everything that had characterised that life: the religion to which his father had devoted himself being always his first target, with all its odious, irrational taboos and restrictions. But he had only negative things to say about the rest, too: to him it seemed to have been all a dreariness, narrowness, slovenliness; rotten with indolence and resentment of anything other than itself; littered with the monuments of misplaced scholarly zeal which the religion had inspired; redeemed only by the promise of escape – escape, above all, to any corner of the English-speaking world. Now, as he had voluntarily brought these pictures to me, and as he evidently did not want to put them away, I thought this might be the opportunity to get him to say something detailed or particular about his past. But he paid no attention to my questions. 'Ach!' he still groaned. 'Ach!' Finally I asked him a direct question about his father, my grandfather, the man missing from the pictures, whose place he had been called on prematurely to fill. What sort of person had he been? That question did produce an answer. 'Benighted!' he said grandly. That was all. I put the photographs in his jacket pocket, and they remained there until the end of the visit. I did not come across them when I gathered his possessions together many weeks later; but I did the job so rapidly that that hardly meant anything. Perhaps they were still in the pocket of his jacket.

The deterioration which set in some time after the episode with the photographs took two forms. First, he came to visit me less often; secondly, when he did come he had less and less to say for himself. He had also begun to run down physically: it showed in his walk, in his eyes, in the constant movements of his tongue inside his closed mouth. He had lost his appetite. He was always in need of a shave. Even his shoes, about which he had been so mysteriously punctilious, no longer shone as before. Sighs and groans were virtually his only utterances now; when he did speak he was inclined to mix up Johannesburg and London, and the headlines of the day with those of a year or two before. I wondered how long he would be able to keep going, and what form the final collapse I was expecting would take.

He managed to surprise me, all the same. Visiting the house one day (it was the last visit of that kind which he was ever to make, though neither of us knew it) he announced that he was going 'on holiday' to Israel. That someone in his condition should have dreamed up such a plan was surprising enough; more surprising still, in a way, was his destination. He had never visited Israel before, and had always spoken of the country with a hostility that had a peculiarly personal element of vexation in it. To him, Israel and the whole Zionist endeavour were nothing more than yet another example of the Jewish passion for self-separation; he seemed to feel that the very existence of the Jewish state was a half-secularised (and all the more insidious, therefore) affront to the universal enlightenment, or enlightened universalism, to which he genuinely believed he had dedicated his intellectual life.

And now he was going there for a holiday. I could not understand it and did not believe him until he showed me his airline ticket and the vouchers he had bought for a fourteen-night stay in a Tel Aviv hotel. Then I had to try to make plausible to myself the idea of his getting to the right terminal at Heathrow Airport, on the right day and at the right time, negotiating the passport and customs checks, and presenting himself at the appropriate boarding-channel for his plane. None of it was easy to imagine. I was relieved to hear that he had arranged for someone to take him to the airport.

But I no more offered to fetch him from it, on his return, than I had pressed him to come more regularly to the house than he was now in the habit of doing. Of course I felt bad about these inner abandonments of him; but doing more for him, I was sure, would have made me feel worse, in other ways. How does one know when one's duty to anyone else is fulfilled? The answer is one never does. One makes up the rules as one goes along, and breaks them as one goes along. Every case is different from every other. I wished him *bon voyage* and told him that I looked forward to hearing what he made of Israel. Who knows, I said in feebly jocular fashion, he might come back converted to the Zionist cause. My uncle's manner had always been humourless, and the drugs he had taken had done nothing to change him in that regard. 'Never,' he said with much seriousness. 'Such a thing is impossible.'

It was May, the crescendo month for growth, light, colour, bird song, rain that left the streets ablaze, playful skies, armies of builders and decorators in splashed white overalls perched on ladders outside suburban homes. I walked some way with him through the suburb, then we cut across a corner of the Heath. The hawthorns were covered so thickly with blossom they looked as if sheets of pink and white had been thrown over them and left to dry, Irish country-fashion. We shook hands when we parted. He was eager to get away.

Eventually I was to learn that he had in fact gone to Israel. But I never found out how he had managed the trip or what he had made of the place. We talked about it only once subsequently, and by then the visit seemed to have gone pretty much out of his mind. All he had to say about it was a vague, uninterested recollection of the flight: 'So quick, nowadays. Amazing really.' We were sitting together on a bench when he said this, in a little enclosure made by a pair of low, U-shaped hedges facing one another across a goldfish pond. There did not seem to be any fish in the pond, among the water-lilies; it would have been difficult to see them, anyway, because the whole thing was covered with close-mesh netting wire.

Whether the netting was there to protect the fish from predatory birds and cats, or to keep the inmates of the institution I was visiting from trying to drown themselves in the pond, I have no way of knowing.

Behind tall brick walls on both sides of a gateway, past wide expanses of turf and a few flower-beds, amid a group of gaunt buildings with windows netted over like the fish-pond, I had found my uncle waiting for me. It was autumn then: not the season of mists and mellow fruitfulness, but, on that day at least, a rather dry, stiff affair, with leaves congregating noisily in gutters and a shallow, expanded sun hanging in the sky. The drive across London to get to the mental hospital in which he was confined had taken hours: some bureaucratic procedure had determined that a man who lived in the north-west of the city should be consigned to a hospital far in the south-east, where London gives way to areas which cannot be called countryside; merely not-London. But since I had been the one who had invoked that bureaucratic procedure, so that I might be relieved of the burden of his life and its manias, I was hardly in a position to complain.

What had happened was this. Two days after the first call I had received from the hospital in Hampstead, there was another. This one, from a clerk in the general office, came early in the morning. He told me baldly that my uncle was expecting me to come and pick him up in an hour's time. Pick him up? To do what with him? Take him home of course, the clerk said, in patient, burly tones, and rang off.

It was still summer, then. The morning air was scented with dew and exhaust fumes. Before leaving for the hospital, I had a brief conference with my wife about whether or not I should bring my uncle back to the house. The conference was brief because neither of us wanted him to come. Among the many tangled emotions I felt about this decision was, inevitably, one of resentment against him for his having obliged me to make it.

I found him pacing up and down the pavement. The street was narrow, a sloping Hampstead defile. To one side was the brick bulk of the hospital; on the other, elevated high above the street, was a pub with an open terrace or platform in front of it. On summer evenings people of a predictable kind gathered there: walkers of their dogs across the Heath and collectors of china, young men in publishing and industrial design, teachers in technical colleges and their physiotherapist girl-friends. A shabbily elegant crowd, with some money but not too much; some intellect but not too much; some freedom from convention but not too much.

My uncle belonged to another world. He was dressed, as always, in one of his old suits: presumably the one in which he had been admitted to the hospital. It was too big for him, now that the shrinking of old age had him remorselessly in its grip. Abraded, patched, wrinkled, gazing anxiously about him, he resembled a child whose mother has providently bought every item of his clothing two sizes too large for him. He came to the car the moment I halted. He came to it with a reproach, not a greeting.

'Where have you been? I've been waiting and waiting.' He opened the back door and climbed in, practically going down on all fours in his eagerness to get away. 'So let's go. You know where to go? You know the way?'

I asked him about his things. 'Yes, my things,' he agreed vaguely, climbing or wallowing about on the back seat. Then, sitting up, thrusting his face close to my own, he was suddenly inflamed. 'What, there's nothing! Just take me away from here!'

I had turned round to speak to him. The more I saw the unhappier I became. It was his tremulousness that worried me most. His eyelashes, nostrils, and lips seemed to be vibrating in front of me; his limbs were more grossly afflicted. He couldn't keep still for a moment. At the same time he was talking, or issuing orders, with a frantic, rambling rapidity. If I didn't take him away at once he'd get a taxi. A man could always get a taxi. I must give him the money to pay for the taxi. Who could believe it, that they'd let a man out of a place like that without a penny in his pocket. He'd told the woman to lend him a couple of pounds, how much was it, she had his name and address, he wouldn't run away with her money. But no! All they knew in there was how to torture you, never to give you anything . . .

And much more of the same sort. Then, in mid-phrase, he had opened the door of the car and was off, his old man's eager gait carrying him to the corner of the High Street. I went after him and grabbed hold of his arm. He gave me a sliding, muddy glance; then set off back to the car as rapidly as he had fled from it. He opened the door and sat down inside, looking at me through the window with the longsuffering expression of a man who doesn't know what all the fuss and delay is about, but is deliberately restraining himself from asking. The only trouble was that the car he was now sitting in was not mine.

I coaxed him out of the stranger's car and got him to sit in the front seat of mine, before going into the hospital. The man at the desk in the main entrance did not have anything to tell me, so I went down to the basement-ward once again. The ward sister I met this time was more sympathetic than the last; it turned out that she was the one who had phoned me originally. She obviously felt that my uncle was not nearly ready to leave, but, she said, they could not stop him from doing so; it was impossible to keep someone in the hospital against his will. No, there was nothing for him to take away: he was wearing the clothes he had come in, and she had put his wallet and glasses in his pocket. And a toothbrush, she added. She also had some medication for him – and here she went through a little collection of pill-containers arranged on her desk, each of which had a kind of paper ruff around its neck, until she found the one she was looking for – which she was rather anxious about. It was most important that he should follow the instructions about taking the pills: one every four hours. She undid the ruff encircling the container and passed it over to me.

Her cool, clean fingers met mine. We exchanged a strange look: one of complete frankness about the fraudulence of the transaction in which we were engaged. My uncle might swallow all the pills at once, or lose them all, or discover them in his pocket days later: one thing certain was that he would not take a pill every four hours.

All else aside, he would never be able to figure out that twelve o'clock, say, was four hours later than eight o'clock, and that pill-taking time had thus come round again.

Without any animosity the ward sister said, 'He hasn't been an easy patient.' She got to her feet, a tall, slender woman, in nun-like garb, and walked a few paces with me to the foot of the stairs. The lift-shaft was silent, breathing out oil and dust; the smudged cream walls and brass-edged steps of the stairway already looked as melancholy as a memory, something from the past. Pronouncing my uncle's name as if it were a difficult foreign word, the sister wished him the best of luck. I went upstairs and found him sitting in the car exactly as I had left him. But he had slowed down a little, which was a relief. His air was now more plaintive than possessed. He had no difficulty in remembering his address.

When I got to his house there followed yet another interview with another strange woman, another paid surrogate for mother or wife; the third of its kind I had had. This one was with his landlady: a well-dressed woman not much younger than my uncle, and about the same height, but much more fleshy. Her shiny, strapped, high-heeled shoes reminded me of spiders, for some reason. Adorned with rings, lace, rouge, blackened eyelashes, and sausage-shaped curls, she occupied the ground floor of the house, and received visitors in an over-furnished living-room-cum-office-cum-shrine. The shrine part of it, which I had time to study only on the visit I was forced to make to the house the next day, was devoted entirely to mementoes of her late husband. There were medals embedded in velvet; framed certificates testifying to his achievements in swimming and mechanical engineering; photographs which showed him with his wife or in the company of other men, in civilian clothes or in the uniform of a Central European army, with rolled-up diplomas in hand or leaning back at a formal dinner. Some of these items were hung on the wall, but most were affixed to a fretted, gabled piece of furniture suitable for no purpose other than the one to which it had been put. It had a tall back and, as it were, no front: projecting from it was just a single drawer, on top of which lay a thick black book that could have been a Bible or a work on mechanical engineering.

It was an impressive display. However, the style of the woman who had organised it was one of fluttery politeness and femininity. This turned into histrionic helplessness once she had had a proper look at my uncle. It was a shock for me, too, to see him in different surroundings from before, away from the context of the hospital. Staring about him uncomprehendingly, dwarfed by his baggy clothes, plasters alternating with purple abrasions on his scratched-up, patched-up face, he looked disastrous. To make things worse, a renewed fit of restlessness had seized him. He twitched, fidgeted, snorted, grimaced, began making little runs in the limited space available between the landlady's pieces of furniture, and suddenly left the room at a trot. We heard him go upstairs and open a door; a moment later he had started to move furniture about. Or so it seemed. Things fell, footsteps sounded back and forth.

The landlady did not let me escape until she had extracted my name and telephone number from me. 'This is a quiet house,' she said. 'I can't bear noisy conditions' – using the word, so far as I could make out, in its medical sense. She would not take the plastic box of pills which the ward sister had given me; hopelessly enough, I had thought she might supervise his taking of them. I went upstairs to my uncle's room, to give the pills to him, and to say goodbye. He met me at the door. His suit was now brightly adorned with three or four letters in red, white and blue airmail envelopes, which he had crammed unopened into the breast-pocket. They were from his children, presumably. I tried to persuade him to get into bed: there it was, occupying almost one half of the long, narrow room; it was even made up, after a fashion. The air was breathlessly stuffy after his long absence, and I opened the window at the other end of the room from the bed. I also looked for a pair of pyjamas in a chest of drawers, found them, and proffered them to him. But he wasn't interested. Why should he get into bed? What was I talking about? It was still broad daylight. He was going for a walk now.

I left the room with the pills in my pocket. The phone was already ringing by the time I got home. It was the landlady telling me to come and fetch my uncle: he was frightening her and disturbing the other lodgers; she wasn't prepared to have him in the house any longer. I spent a good part of that day either on the telephone or in the motor car; among other things I went back to his room and tried to persuade him to return to the hospital. It was only after I had failed in that attempt that I decided I was going to try to have him committed, legally committed, to a mental hospital. The fact that it was a Friday, and that the weekend had just about begun, did not make it easier to have him examined.

The following morning there gathered in the landlady's living-room an undersized psychiatrist in a brown suit, a female psychiatric social worker (both of whom were employed by the Borough), and myself. Apparently their signatures would be sufficient to secure a committal. The social worker had a clipboard on her lap and a pencil in her hand; she was a very young girl in a blue dress with white spots; her fair, straight hair, which hung down to her collar, was newly washed. The psychiatrist sat in silence, looking at his shoes, which were no great distance from his eyes, or at the ceiling. The landlady put her head around the door every now and again. Upstairs my uncle still seemed to be moving furniture about: less noisily than on the previous day, but pretty continuously nevertheless.

Nothing could have made the meeting anything but a painful one. The psychiatrist did his best to prolong it, and to exacerbate its unpleasantness. Of all those I met who were paid for what they did in relation to my uncle, he was the only one whom I felt to be actively hostile to me. Even the first of the ward sisters I had spoken to had not been hostile; merely bossy and indifferent. This man, whose responsibility for my uncle's welfare would end with his putting a signature to a piece of paper, or refusing to do so, had it in for me. Whether out of libertarian sentiment, or out of resentment at having his Saturday morning spoiled, he was determined to make me as uncomfortable, morally speaking, as he could. 'We're not going to put your uncle in a mental hospital for your convenience,' he said several times: a remark to which I had no reply, since it was indeed partly for my own convenience that I was trying to arrange to have him put there. 'Where do you want him to go?' I asked, but he dismissed the question. 'That isn't the issue.' The social worker sat with her eyes cast down, busily shading with her pencil a small area of the paper clipped to the board on her lap. She had a sympathetic manner, but clearly the psychiatrist, with his red face and sharp nose turned up to the ceiling, was the one who counted.

At one time he sent the social worker to bring my uncle downstairs. The noises we had heard from upstairs had led me to think he would be in a frenzied state; but it was as if he knew, once he had entered the room, that he was in the presence of an authority different from those he had encountered before. He was quiet and docile, like a bewildered child. I had never felt so acutely how much the whole pattern of his life had come to resemble a luridly fore-shortened and doubled over version of what we all have to go through, eventually, if we live long enough. He had been hardly more than a child when, with a child's zeal, he had adopted the role of the adult: he had been father to his siblings and husband to his mother long before he had married and fathered his own children; later he had even made a profession of being a father (or secular rabbi!) outside the home. Now he sat on a couch between a psychiatrist and a girl younger than his own daughter, childishly anxious to do whatever they wanted of him. The only trouble was that he simply could not manage the difficult, grown-up tasks they set him. They asked him what day of the week it was, and he did not know. They asked him the name of his landlady, and he could not tell them. They asked him how long he had been out of the hospital, and he could not remember being in it, let alone leaving it. His voice became hoarser and hoarser with each failure; his demeanour more bewildered. He did not look up at all. What kind of inquisition was this that he was being put through? What were these strangers really after? Couldn't they see how unfair they were being? Questions like these were visible, as it were, in the lines of his neck and shoulders, and in the slow movements of his hands in his lap. Finally he fell silent; he would answer no more questions; they could do what they liked with him. Only his hands continued to move, to twist and rub against one another. The sound was quite audible in the silence of the room.

The social worker took him upstairs, like a child who had failed to perform adequately. The psychiatrist took some papers out of his brief-case and consulted them. It was during this lull that I had the opportunity of studying the landlady's shrine to her late husband. The social worker returned, and the strange bumping noises from upstairs recommenced. The landlady made one of her periodic appearances. The psychiatrist asked me to leave the room, so that he might phone ('in confidence') my uncle's general practitioner. I waited in the hallway outside. He came out of the room a little later and told me that he was going to interview my uncle again, upstairs, away from what he called 'other influences'. He threw a look in my direction on the last phrase. It seemed that not only did I wish to lock up my uncle for my own convenience; I was also in the business of terrorising him (literally) out of his wits.

Apparently my uncle did no better away from those 'other influences' than he had done in their presence. But he was noisier: we could hear his raised, angry tones, though none of the words he used. The psychiatrist came downstairs and entered into a conversation with the social worker about summoning an ambulance. The possibility of alerting the police in case of 'resistance' was also mentioned. The social worker offered to drive my uncle to the hospital in her car, if he was agreeable. The psychiatrist signed various papers from among those he had put out on the table, and the social worker put her name under his. Then she clipped copies of the papers to her board. It had been done. He had been committed.

He offered no resistance to being taken away by car. The last glimpse I had of him that morning was in the passenger seat of the social worker's Ford Escort. Herself like a child playing grown-ups, her hair fallen forward across her face, she was absorbedly leaning over him to fasten his safety belt. Once they had gone, the psychiatrist left in his car. He did not say goodbye to me or to the landlady. I promised the latter that I would return shortly to clear my uncle's stuff from the room.

It was noon by the time I left the house. Under a sky of sunshine and vague cloud the streets were crowded with people going about the tasks they had had no time for during the week: buying groceries, visiting launderettes and public libraries, having their hair done, taking their children to shoe-shops.

Among the suits, ties, socks, folders of letters, grey flannel trousers, transistor radios (two), and the rest of the stuff which I threw into the suitcases I found in my uncle's room, and into the boxes I had brought with me, was the book I mentioned at the beginning of this memoir. I did not know what it was; it struck me at the time solely because it was the only book in Hebrew in the entire collection. It went into a box on top of all the others: among them Arthur Koestler on the nature of scientific discovery, Frazer's *Golden Bough* in the abbreviated, two-volume edition, *The Rationalist Annual* of the previous year's date, an inscribed copy of one of my own novels.

It was all quick and easy enough. My uncle did not have that many possessions, after all. However, he did have a plentiful supply of 'certain articles', as he was to describe them many weeks later, that were a problem to me. In clearing up I came across a multitude of glass and plastic containers of pills and capsules of all shapes, sizes, and colours: mostly white, of course, but also blue, red, red-and-white, mottled pink, purple, green. There must have been many hundreds of pills in the collection. Most of the names on the containers meant nothing to me. What was I to do with them? After some hesitation I put them all in a big plastic bag, which I took downstairs and threw into a rubbish-bin standing in a passageway to the side of the house. Subsequently I was to feel it had been officious of me to have acted in this way. I also learned subsequently that I had not followed the approved procedure for disposing of unwanted pills: one should flush them down the lavatory.

Anyway, these pills were hardly 'unwanted'. My uncle wanted them. Many weeks later, on his discharge from the mental hospital, the very first thing he did was to look for them among his belongings. He was extremely disappointed not to find them. I know this because I was with him, in the room in my house where his stuff was stored, when he discovered the loss he had suffered. He did not speak of the pills as such, of course; not by name. All he did was to hunt rapidly through the bags and boxes, then to go through them a second time, rather more slowly, then to ask me if I was sure that everything I had brought from the room was there. I assured him that it was. 'Funny,' he said. 'There are certain articles missing. I can't understand it.' Another search yielded nothing; nor did the further, vague, euphemistic questions he put to me. I wasn't prepared to confess to him what I had done. Thereupon, though all the way from the hospital he had been insisting that before proceeding on the next stage of the journey it was absolutely necessary for him to 'sort out' his things, he lost interest in them completely.

It must have been about three or four weeks after my first visit to the mental hospital that I went there to bring him away. He had been discharged with the full agreement of the hospital authorities; his daughter was due to return from the States shortly; in the meantime he would stay with a childless couple, distantly related to him and to me, who were about the same age as himself. I had intended taking him straight from the hospital to their flat in Kensington, but he would not hear of it. He had to sort out his things first. Strangely enough, it had not even occurred to me, when I made the detour to my house, as he had requested, that his pills were what he was really after.

We stood in the room with the open bags and boxes around us. I tried to press on him some of the other articles that were lying around: didn't he want to take this sweater, that pair of shoes, these vests and underpants? No, he did not. Insistent though he had been in the car, his manner had also been very remote. Every remark I made had seemed to take a long time to reach him, and everything he said also seemed to have to travel a great distance to come out. At one point, I remember, he said, 'The trouble with society nowadays is that it's too complicated; too much is expected of people; if they can't cope they punish them' – and I was filled with the eerie conviction that he was referring to the cross-examination about days of the week and the name of his landlady to which he had been subjected on the morning of his committal. Now, in the disappointment of not finding his pills, he seemed to retreat even farther than before; it was as if he would never have occasion to speak to me again. My eye fell on that odd-shaped, solitary, shabby Hebrew book lying on top of others in a box. To try to rouse him, to bring him back as it were, I picked up the book and asked him, 'What is this?'

He looked at it in my hand. I would not have been surprised, if he had not answered at all. Eventually he said, 'That? That's a collection of my grandfather's writings – so-called. It's terrible stuff. Absolutely worthless. Talmudic *pilpul* (hair-splitting), all of it. He knew nothing else, poor man.'

I opened the torn cover of the book and looked at the faded photograph which made up the frontispiece: an old man with a grey beard and a steep-sided skull-cap fitting wholly over the top of his head. His beard was so ragged at the ends it looked like some kind of hanging moss. Faded and blurrily reproduced though the picture was, I could see my uncle in the man's bald brow and broad, fleshy nose; or the old man in these features of my uncle. It was all one.

My uncle said, 'Do you want the book? You can have it. With my compliments.'

That was how it came into my possession. It is a book that only a devout student of the Talmud could read. That is a literal observation, not a literary one. It is printed in a special Hebrew script ('the Rashi script') which was used specifically for works of this nature, and which it is difficult even for someone who knows the ordinary, square Hebrew alphabet to penetrate. Moreover, there is hardly a sentence in the book which is not crowded with references – references so abbreviated as to be in effect a private code reserved for scholars like the author himself – to chapters and verses in the Bible, and to rulings and discussions in various tractates of the Talmud and its different recensions. For all I can make out of the one hundred and eighty-four large, double-columned, closely printed pages of the book, it might as well be written in cuneiform or some other packed, ghostly script like it.

The title-page and the introduction are, however, in conventional Hebrew characters. They can be read by anyone who has a modicum of the language. This (in translation) is what the title-page says, and how it is laid out:

BOOK
ZVI (GENIUS) YA'AKOV
Questions and Answers, Interpretations and
Explanations, in the Order of the Talmud
and the Commentaries

BY

The Honoured Master and Teacher, the Great and True
Genius, the Prince of the Torah and the Storehouse
of Light, a Lion among his Companions, the Righteous
and Everlasting Upholder of Truth, the Deer of Israel
and the Genius of Jacob, Our Instructor and Rabbi,
ZVI YA'AKOV OPPENHEIM of Saintly and Blessed Memory,
Sometime President of the Rabbinical Court of
Kelme (Lithuania).

Published by the supplier of Books from the
House of the Widow of Rabbi Hotnauer (of
Blessed Memory), Teacher of Righteousness,
24 Franziskana, Warsaw, Poland.

Printed in Letland 1920

There then follows the introduction or blurb.

ZVI THE RIGHTEOUS ONE

The son must honour the father, and the student his teacher. So as we approach the task of bringing forth this wonderful book, the child of our master's mind, it is right for us to declare from generation to generation his greatness, and to describe his loftiness of spirit, and to proclaim on this gateway the righteousness and wisdom to which it serves as entrance.

This book brings together but little of the sayings of his lips and the writings of his hand, which gave such comfort to those who thirsted for his words. Much was lost through the evils and calamities which came upon us. The failings of the book spring also from ZVI YA'AKOV's indifference to his own writings, in comparison with his zeal to do the work of God and to bring the light to Israel. Most of what we have gathered together was written only as brief notes for himself. We have dared to present these fragments because they are all that has been left behind by ZVI YA'AKOV, the wonder of Israel.

He was born of one of the most highly connected families in Israel, the OPPENHEIMS, who for many generations had been labouring for the Torah. His father, the Master of the Torah, was Rabbi MICHAEL YITZHAK, of blessed and pious memory, and his modest and dutiful mother was TSIPPE, of blessed memory. Even in his childhood he revealed his wonderful talents, like a prodigy, and before he had completed his ninth year he was studying Gemara [commentaries on the Talmud] without the aid of a teacher. He came to warm himself at the great light of Rabbi LEVI SHAPIRA in Trischik, who included in his book, 'The House of Levy' some interpretations of the Torah made when he was only eleven years old. . . .

And so on and so on. Some human detail is added: such as the fact that at times Zvi Ya'akov would draw both the shutters and the curtains of his room 'in order not to be distracted by those passing to and fro outside', and would spend a whole day and a night studying incessantly by the light of a single candle; during the more joyous festivals and holy days, on the other hand, he would make merry with the boys from the Talmud school 'and even with infants'. No indication is given of the date of his death, though the contrast is repeatedly drawn between the strength of his devotion to the Law ('like iron') and the weakness of his bodily frame. At the end of the introduction a host of nephews, nieces, cousins, brothers-in-law, sons-in-law and others, most of them in Lithuania, one or two in Brooklyn, New York, come in for a flattering mention. Some of these are delicately thanked, it would seem, for contributing funds which made possible the printing of the book. Finally there is a request to those who wish for further copies of it to write not to the printer but directly to Benne Oppenheim, the author's son in Kelme. He was evidently the one who was responsible for bringing out the compilation.

Twenty-three years after he had completed his work, the German troops who were occupying Kelme during the Second World War gathered together in the town's synagogue what was left of its Jewish community. The doors were locked, the building was doused with petrol, and it was set alight.

Among those who died in the blaze were Benne, who must have been an old man by then, two of his sisters, and their husbands. All their children died with them.

My mother had told me in the vaguest terms what had happened to that part of her family which had remained in Lithuania. I suspect that her vagueness had sprung from a desire to protect her own feelings rather than mine. It was from one of my aunts, on a visit to South Africa that took place long after the events I have described here, that I learned the story.

By that time my uncle, too, was dead. It is remarkable how seldom I saw him after the day he gave the copy of Zvi Ya'akov's book to me. The last time we were alone together, in fact, was when I drove him to the people with whom he was to stay. On our arrival his hosts came out on to the pavement; while we talked, in a street buffeted by the wind and noisy with fallen leaves, they surreptitiously eyed him, trying to size up the task they had taken on in inviting him into their house. I think they were reassured by what they saw. My uncle, though still remote in manner, was quite matter-of-fact about his being there and his status as their guest. I declined their suggestion that I should come in for a cup of tea. One topic of conversation that came up, I remember, was the disease called 'scrapie', which attacks sheep; the wife was doing research on it in the institution which employed her.

I do not think I saw my uncle more than three or four times in the years that followed. When his daughter and her husband returned, he went to live with them in the house they had bought in the country. There he remained until the end of his life, which came seven or eight years later. He never 'recovered'; he never, so far as I know, suffered a collapse as thoroughgoing as the one I had witnessed. He was looked after with much devotion by his daughter and son-in-law. In return he helped around the house; he did some baby-sitting when he was up to it, and some fetching of the children from school; he went for long walks.

The last time we met was in the company of my brother, who was visiting from South Africa, and was especially keen to see him once more. We went for a drive on that occasion, too: one of a very different kind from the last I had taken with him. Following the instructions we had been given, the three of us drove to a village a few miles away, parked the car, and passed through a gate to one side of the village churchyard. We followed a path alongside hedgerows for some distance, and suddenly, around a turning, there it was, the view we had been recommended to find: a small, placid river, a wooden footbridge over it, elm trees rising to a great height from the fields nearby, and more distant trees seeming to browse on the late afternoon light, the masses of their leaves making up not one horizon, but many horizons, in the direction both from which the water came and that towards which it was going. No other people were about. Everything stirred – the dark water plucking at the supports of the bridge, the flags that grew along the bank, the leaves on the trees, the sheen on the grass – and everything was still, poised, calm, settled, perfectly in place. We spent some time there. On the way back my uncle burst out, his cheeks curiously puffed and his eyes squeezed shut, as if it was impossible for him to contain the words any longer, 'I never expected to live so long.'

It was the nearest he ever came, at least in my presence, to explaining himself. The next time I went up that way it was to attend his cremation. There was no religious ceremony of course; only music, and a few thoughtful, candid words of praise by some-one who had known him in Johannesburg. Then machines hummed and the coffin passed out of sight.

LAST HOME
HOLIDAY

There was no such thing, it seemed, as the passage of time. The glittering iron roof of the house; the grape vine's shadow on the back verandah; the weariness of late afternoons, when Namaqua doves called from the silver oak in the corner of the garden; flat streets lined with heat-shrivelled trees and bounded on every horizon by blue-green dumps of treated soil from the diamond mines; above all, the sky unchanging in its slow, repeated changes, as stormclouds gathered in columns and toppling castles and lazy continents, and dissipated with no discharge of rain, until at last the stars came out – nothing had altered, what was there that could alter? The cracks in the polished, red-dyed cement of the verandah were like fissures in my brain; even the sag of a particular cushion on a chair, or the sound of a motor bike drilling through the stillness, was as much a recollection as a perception, a discovery not so much of something out there as of something that had always been within me. Every scent, every shadow and gleam or flare of light, every irregularity touched by hand or feet, was trance-like in its insistence on being what it always had been.

So time was absent; as if it had done away with itself. Yet there was nothing around me other than the depredations of time. Time lived through us or on us as a flame lives on the wood it consumes and chars; we were what it charred and turned to ash. Invisible flame, more powerful even than the sun! The dead, my mother first among them, were gone; sky, streets, and cushions bore no trace of them; the air was empty of them; the house was not inhabited by their ghosts. On pavements, outside the shops I visited in town, eyes encaged in wrinkles met mine in mutual recognition; schoolyard bullies, once-desired girls in gym slips, Africans who had worked for families no longer to be seen, scanned all that time had done to me, as I scanned their grey or bald heads, shrivelled complexions, thicknesses and emaciations that could never have been predicted. We were all caught equally in one embrace, from which we could escape only by being delivered of everything we had known: body, mind, world.

My father shuffled down the passage to his bedroom. He was afflicted with palsy in his right arm, crippled by rheumatism, ravaged by the eighty-eight years of his life. He could no longer cut his own meat, he had difficulty in bringing his fork to his lips, his memory was erratic, his hearing thick. He slept badly, at irregular hours; it was a great effort for him to get out of an armchair. There were hours, on certain days, when he was talkative, malicious, self-deceiving, full of improbable plans for the future: killings he intended to make in real estate deals; arguments he was going to have with the well-counted ranks of his enemies, living and dead; scores he had to settle with the Russians who threatened the wellbeing of the State of Israel or with his sons who hadn't done with their lives just what he had intended them to do. On these mornings he read *The Diamond Fields Advertiser*; he listened to the news on the radio, though he would immediately forget what he had heard; he would insist on being driven down to the business he still believed he ran, the last of the many enterprises he had launched, where he sat behind his empty desk for an hour or two before being driven home again. But there were also days when he would be unable to leave his bedroom, and could not tell morning from afternoon, and had difficulty in remembering which of his sons I was.

He still appears in my dreams in that form: his neck and arms shrunken; his ankles enlarged; heelless, torn slippers on his feet; the fringes of his underpants thrusting out beneath the single pair of flannel trousers he always wore, as often as not with a pyjama jacket above; his mouth pursed forward and hanging to one side;

his eyes alert and bewildered; someone about to be abandoned once again to the sprawling solitude of his five bedrooms, three living rooms, two dark, malodorous bathrooms, long, high-ceilinged passages, a cement verandah back and front, a large garden reverting to so much hot sand, an orchard at the back, together with garage, shed, servants' quarters. Once all this had housed himself, his wife, his three sons, his daughter, at least two and sometimes three full-time servants. Now the rooms were for him and the one remaining servant alone. There were taps that did not run; electric lights which could not be switched on; an abandoned stove standing in a corner of the back verandah; an out-of-action refrigerator in the passage, parked alongside another which clattered and rumbled all night through, and which had not been defrosted for years; an entire bookcase full of steam-buckled books in one of the bathrooms. Empty, no-longer-worn suits – striped suits, summer suits, formal suits – hung in wardrobes above unused pairs of shoes; old letters and invoices lay in cardboard boxes, where they had lain for years, along with photographs and copies of *The South African Jewish Times* which had never been taken out of their wrappers.

I had come back to South Africa from London for three weeks; as much time as I could spare, or felt I could spare, from wife, children, work, the life I had made overseas. For twenty years I had been coming back at intervals to the house and the town in which I had grown up; occasionally my father had visited us in London; now he could travel no longer. It was December, midsummer. By day the heat and light outside were nothing less than grandiose; at night the dark stillness was stifling. I suspected (rightly, as things turned out) that this was the last such journey I would make. On some of the previous trips I had been accompanied by my family; but not on this occasion. Previously my father had spoken as though it were possible that either I or one of his other children, all of whom had left the town, would return to Kimberley, not for a holiday, but for good. This time, however, he did not speak of that hope; he expected nothing of us. We had let him down, finally. He was on his own.

Well, not quite on his own. Being so weak and so subject to confusion, he could not have managed alone for more than a day or two. Betty was still with him. She had worked for my parents for many years; then for my father alone even longer. She lived in the room across the back yard where she had always lived; a bell had been rigged up so that he could call her if he needed help at any time. Once or twice a week an African labourer came to do such work around the house as Betty herself could no longer do, or no longer wanted to do: polishing the floors, tidying up what was left of the garden. For the period of my stay – Betty had a free hand in such matters – she had also hired a full-time assistant, an African girl, Rebecca by name. Rebecca was many years younger than Betty; she had a cast in her eye, which gave her a somewhat wanton look, and a bold, straight-backed way of carrying herself. To Betty she spoke in Xhosa; to me in Afrikaans; of the two of us it was towards Betty that she adopted the more respectful demeanour, on the whole.

Betty must have been in her mid-fifties at the time; perhaps a little older. Her face was flat, smooth-browed, pale brown in colour; her eyes were faintly Oriental in shape and tilt; on her head she wore a close-fitting cap with an elasticated rim and a floral pattern printed on it, though on formal occasions she would don a white, starched affair, something like a nurse's. Her body was broad and thick, though not nearly as much of either as it had been when she had come to work for my parents a couple of decades before. Her legs, which were darker in colour than her face, were swollen and scarred; on her feet, invariably, was an ancient pair of sandals. She used her hands, pale palms and finger alike, in extensive gestures when she spoke. Unlike most of the domestic servants who had been in the house during my childhood, she preferred to speak English to us, rather than Afrikaans. Her English was often of a rather elevated kind. She never ran in a bath for my father, for example; she always 'drew' it. She was an expert at folding table napkins into the shape of starched crowns; she was a practiced flower-arranger and silver-polisher, as well as an excellent cook. These genteel accomplishments were not her only skills. She also served, in effect, as my father's nurse, for she helped him to bathe and to dress, massaged his ankles when they were especially painful, gave him her arm when he was too weak to walk up and down the passage unaided. She ordered meat and fish and groceries by telephone, and bickered over fruit and vegetables with an Indian hawker who brought a van round to the house. The household accounts were paid from the business, since my father could no longer make out a cheque: his hand shook too much, and in any case he found figures of any kind especially confusing.

Thus his physical and domestic wellbeing were wholly in Betty's hands. About this he felt no sense of shame, or even any special sense of obligation towards her, fond though he was of her. She was his servant. He paid her. She was black. She lived in a room across the back yard of the house. She called him 'Master'. So why should he feel anything she did for him to be a derogation of his dignity?

Have no fear, she got her own back on him. A ramshackle, lovingly vindictive version of the entire history of South Africa stood behind and within the relationship between the two of them. She was devoted to him; she would spend hours with him by day and night, talking to him or merely sitting by his bedside in order to calm him simply by her presence. She could also be a devious drunken, hemp-smoking blackmailer, who knew just how much power she had over him, and who enjoyed using it. A favourite trick of hers was to frighten him reasonlessly: one day it might be with the announcement that 'they' were coming to cut off the water; another that she had distinctly heard burglars and '*skollie*-boys' in the house next door. All the servants she hired for one temporary job or another, Rebecca not excluded, had their reputations thoroughly blackened before they were discharged. Though she could hardly get rid of them in quite the same way, she made many insidious suggestions to my father about my brothers and sister, and their children. Everything she said, he believed – for a while at least. The more he believed, the more she laid it on.

The relationship between the two of them was archaic, perhaps unimaginable elsewhere; one would have had to go to the literature of Tsarist Russia, to Gogol or Herzen or some of the tales of Tolstoy, to find parallels to its absurdity and intimacy, the depths of the affection and social distance it spanned, the mutual dependencies and assumptions of superiority, the strange combinations of slyness and candour, that marked every aspect of it. One night, quietly and almost casually, with an emphasis given to her words only by the sound of two fingers slapping against the open palm of the other, and a slightly labouring note in her voice, Betty said to me, 'You mustn't worry. I will stay with the old master to the end. To the very end. God's my witness I'll look after him until he needs me no more.' I believed her, and I was right to believe her. The very next night, however, she was as doped and as drunk as I was to see her during the whole three weeks of my stay, Christmas and New Year aside. (Of those festivals, more below.) She wandered about the house in a random manner, exclaiming, 'Precious!' whenever she saw me; she put into the refrigerator the bottle of whiskey which she had taken from the breakfast room sideboard, and to which she had been helping herself, and put the day's delivery of milk in the sideboard; she ceremoniously hung a kitchen cloth over the back of one of the armchairs in the sitting room, like an antimacassar; eventually I found that she had passed out completely on my bed. Roused with difficulty from there, she prepared the evening meal by placing a can of salmon and a can opener in the very middle of the dining-table, and then disappeared for something like twelve hours. When she returned it was in a head-hanging, penitential fury of polishing, cooking, massaging, ironing, the lot.

Whereupon my father decided to give her a severe talking-to. 'You were drunk again last night,' he told her, one eye cocked at her over a pointing finger. 'I can't understand it. You're a respectable woman. You lack for nothing in this house. I never raise my voice to you. All the neighbours know who you are, and tell me how lucky I am that I have you to look after me. So why do you disgrace yourself like this, in front of me and everyone else?' And much more in the same vein. To all this Betty listened with downcast, inflamed, hungover eyes and sullen, slumped shoulders. At the moment she evidently deemed to be the appropriate one for a change of tactic, she began to snivel. Then to cry more loudly. My father, too, was overcome with emotion. His eye moistened. Also, a certain misgiving that he might be overdoing it, and that Betty might repay him by some even more provocative piece of misbehaviour in the future, began to affect him. So he concluded with a few ingratiating words of commendation. In the end, the insincere protestation that she would never do it again came from him, not from her. Then he told her to go.

Betty obeyed without protest. Some time later she and Rebecca were to be heard in animated conversation in the kitchen. Later still, when I go into the kitchen, I find three solemn white children, whom I have never seen before, seated around the table. They are all girls; they all have straight, flaxen hair coming down to their shoulders, and smooth, tanned complexions; the oldest of them is about ten years old. Betty is feeding them biscuits of her own manufacture. It turns out that they are the children of a house further up the block, and that they often come to pass the time of day with her and to eat her biscuits. The oldest of them is wearing a white t-shirt on which, with a felt-tip pen, she has painstakingly inked in the names of several pop groups, a message declaring to the world, 'I'm my momma's big problem', and the emblem of the nuclear disarmament movement. When I ask her if she knows what the emblem means, she answers without hesitation, her mouth full of crumbs, 'Ban the bomb!' (Or, as her South African vowels would have it, 'Ben the bawm!') However, my intrusion has un-settled them all, and a few minutes later I see the girls trooping across the back yard, on their way out. In the hands of each one is a further supply of biscuits; on their lips sweet cries of farewell, as if they are about to go on a long journey. 'Goodbye Betty! Good-bye!' For her part, Betty stands on the back stoep, the very model, in her apron and cap, of the kindly, much-loved servant, provider of sweetmeats and folk-wisdom, and calls out to them a heartfelt, 'Goodbye, my darlings!'

Needless to say, Betty and the slant-staring, insinuating Rebecca had a number of other visitors during my stay; every now and again there would be a sociable coming and going of people of both sexes and all ages across the yard. These visitors were of course all black. Only once did Betty actually ask me to meet one of them. It was in the evening; the man was waiting for me, deferentially enough, in the back yard. Though a thin moon was up, and the electric light on the verandah had been switched on, all I could see of him was that he was not young, that he was about my height, that his clothing was shabby, that his shoulders had an obliging tilt to them. His features I could not make out at all. Betty introduced me to him, and told me his name; then, while we were shaking hands, she added proudly, so that I might understand just why she had wanted me to meet her distinguished guest, 'He's a sergeant in the Special Branch.' 'A sergeant in the Special Branch?' I repeated in astonishment, my hand still in his. 'Yes sah,' the man answered with a quasi-military jerk of the head and a flash of teeth and eyeball, to indicate that he was indeed a member of the much-feared, ubiquitous, political police, the shock troops (as it were) of the government's *apartheid* policies. 'You're a friend of Betty's?' 'Good friend, sah.' 'Oh.' We stood there. As far as I was concerned I felt there to be no threat from him. No doubt he had reported my presence in the town to his superiors; but so what? It had been in the local paper, anyway. I had no political purposes in making this visit. We exchanged remarks about the hot weather and the prospects for rain. Then I went inside the house and rejoined my father, who was sitting beside the radio in the living room. Supposedly he was listening to the news on the BBC Overseas service. A great susurration, with a whine along its edges, was coming from the machine; in the depths of all this a voice was muttering incomprehensibly.

That voice on his defective radio was as much of a visitor as my father received during my stay. Even as a younger man he had never had all that many friends in the town; now, those he had had were dead or had moved away. Only one friend from my school-days came to see me; I had been away for far too long to expect anything else. So I passed the time by serving as an audience for my father's random monologues, or in reading, or in carrying on with some of the work I had brought with me. There was nothing I could do down at the business, which, though it still employed two whites and about a dozen blacks, had become a mere pretence, an expensive delusion which was somehow necessary to my father's notion of himself. Occasionally I took the car, which nobody else used, and went to the swimming bath, or simply drove it about, among the withered streets of the town, immersed in a dreamlike world of glaring sunlight and heavy shadow which represented myself to myself more deeply than anything I had seen or felt since; and from which, at the same time, I felt myself to be utterly sundered. The streets were so flat, and were bordered by such small trees, and such low corrugated iron roofs and fences, that everything I saw, even the mine dumps, appeared to be at no more than forehead-level – insignificant, tinny, drab, squat. Yet above there rose the naked immensity of the sky. Every day the sun revealed it anew; every night the moon laboured unsuccessfully to reach its summit.

Sometimes my father would talk until quite late at night; it was often from about nine in the evening onwards, in the living room, next to his radio, that he was at his most lively. On the walls were the pictures that had always been there; on the bookshelves were the books they had always carried; on the white, old-fashioned, colonial-style, pressed-steel ceiling was a pattern of Grecian wreaths and ribboned torches that seemed to look at me, rather than be looked at by me. Many of my father's stories I had, inevitably, heard from him before; most of them were about his child-hood in Latvia, which he had left, on his own, at the age of fifteen. Listening to him I found myself wondering to what extent it was the sense I had always had of his having come from another world, and of his having had to fight his way through this one, that had determined my own migration, once I had come of age. All differences allowed for, in settling in England, and making my life there, and thus 'returning' to Europe, had I not been imitating him and competing with him – the two activities which are contained in the very concept of emulation?

One story he told me during that holiday, however, was new to me. It concerned an uncle of his, a man who lived in the same village in Latvia and who had had the reputation of being something of an intellectual in that narrow society: a freethinker, a newspaper reader, a man who owned secular books in Russian and German. This uncle got married when my father was about ten years old. The wedding was a big affair by local standards. When the ceremony was over, the newlyweds drove off in a sleigh, along the snow-covered main road out of the village. In the general excitement of the occasion, a crowd of boys, my father among them, ran alongside the sleigh; then, eager as he was, at every age, to stand out among his companions, and presuming no doubt on the relationship between himself and his uncle, my father went further; he jumped on the back of the sleigh, intending to ride on it for a hundred yards or so, while the others ran alongside.

Almost eighty years later, sitting in one of the front rooms of our iron-roofed house in Kimberley, with the French windows open to the warm stillness and darkness outside, while moths and other furry or long-legged insects ticked against the electric light, I could picture the scene, or try to: the snow of the roadway scarred by tracks, the untouched whiteness beyond, the smell of the horses and the noises they made, the cries of the children, the provinicial or plebeian mirth of the occasion. And my father, a boy of ten (could I picture him?) – small for his age, like any other ill-nourished urchin, in threadbare coat and a cap perhaps too large for him, jumping on the sleigh, which must have given only slightly under the weight of this extra passenger. My father called his uncle by name, and the uncle, the newlywed, who was in charge of the sleigh and had his bride at his side, turned and saw the passenger he had acquired. Without a word, without hesitation, he lashed out with the whip in his hand, and caught my father with it across the neck and cheek.

At this point in his telling of the story, his voice thickened and he found it difficult to carry on. There were tears in his eyes. He drew his hand across his neck, under the ear, and down the side of the cheek, to show me where the whip had left its mark. In the shock and pain of the blow he had fallen off the sleigh and sprawled full-length in the road. The other children laughed. Eighty years later, at the other end of the world, with his left hand to his cheek and his right hand shaking yet inert, inert yet shaking, he earnestly asked me, as if I could give an answer to his questions, as if such questions could be answered anywhere, 'What sort of a man would do such a thing to a little boy? To his own brother's child? And even if I hadn't been family, if I'd been a little peasant boy, how could he bring himself to do it? On his wedding day, in front of his wife?'

The uncle was long dead in his grave in Eastern Europe; my father shuffled down the passage to his bed. Another day of the holiday was over. A few more to go and it would be Christmas. It was to fall on a Monday that year; the following day would be Boxing Day; the shops were to close at Saturday noon. I consulted with Betty well in advance about what we would need for the long weekend. Armed with the shopping list we had jointly drawn up, I went to town and did the shopping on the Friday afternoon. By Kimberley standards the shops were full, even frantic. I bought everything Betty had instructed me to get: the fish we would have ('boiled, with milk') one night; the roast we would have on Christmas Day; the noodles for the macaroni cheese she was planning for another meal; the soup meat, the extra bread and vegetables. The open market in the middle of town was aswarm with Afrikaner farmers and their wives and their pick-up trucks, Indian hawkers, bargaining townsfolk, copper-skinned, tattered, emaciated beggars of quite unfathomable racial origin, black urchins who would carry your bags. On granite slabs next to the reach-me-down Corinthian pillars of the old Town Hall, watermelons and *sponspeks* were piled high in green and scaly-gold pyramids; there were chickens in crates, piles of squashes and pumpkins, plateaus of green and purple grapes, openwork bags of green peas and of carrots as red and angular and jostlingly protruberant as lobsters. How was it that I had passed through this scene innumerable times during my youth and seen in it only the small-town drabness and confusion from which it was imperative for me to escape; that I had never once realised the market to be . . . *picturesque?*

Laden with sufficient goods to be certain that the four of us would not go hungry, and much impressed with the thoroughness of Betty's planning for the occasion, I returned to the house to find my father in a state of alarm. Where had I been? The place was empty. He had been abandoned. How could we have left him alone for hours on end? Thus I discovered that Betty, the planner and home economist, had disappeared. So had Rebecca. Goodbye. They did not return until late afternoon on Boxing Day. Heaven knows where they had caroused the festival away; they never told me. During those days my father and I had got by chiefly on eggs and tinned food and bread. I would have done some cooking – I had nothing else to do – but I simply could not figure out how the various parts of the ancient electric cooker could be got to work, and I was unable to find the places where Betty secreted such elementary things as flour, oil, and cooking salt. The system she operated, if there was one, was beyond me. She returned without any display of contrition or of anxiety about how we had fared in her absence; since we had not witnessed what she had been up to, she evidently felt she had nothing to feel guilty about. But she did prepare a particularly elaborate meal for us on the night of her return, and put out the best linen and plates, which were to reappear only on the night of my departure. This by way of recompense, presumably.

That night I tried to phone London – whether to allay or to exacerbate my own sense of dislocation and futility in the midst of

all this, I do not know. What I do know was that the family in
London for which I was directly responsible had by then become
hardly more real to me than the vestiges of the family for which
my father had been responsible and to which I had once belonged.
In order to make my call, I had first to get through to the international operator in Cape Town. (This was before the days of
international dialled calls.) The operator told me that he would
call me back in due course; there was bound to be a delay at that
time of year; he had five calls to England from Kimberley alone
ahead of me in the queue. Five calls! I could hardly believe it. At
that hour of night? From a dusty nowhere of a place on the edge of
the desert, like Kimberley? And there I had been, flattering myself
with the thought that my life, my circumstances, my preoccupations, my dislocations, were something special, or improbable, or
even singular! In fact I was just another statistic.

A few more days went by and another holiday approached: New
Year's Day. Again it fell on a long weekend. This time I was not
to be fooled by Betty's elaborate preparations, or pretence at
preparations. I did the shopping strictly with my own convenience
in mind, on the assumption that she and her friend would disappear. But she fooled me once again. On the day before the holiday,
Betty cooked and served a midday meal in the normal fashion. In
the afternoon she and Rebecca entertained some of their friends in
their rooms, in a quiet, conversational manner. The evening meal
went off without incident, apart from some bird-like whooping
from the back yard. The sound was loud enough to penetrate even
my father's thick hearing. He looked up from his plate, with a look
that was simultaneously wary, tense, and drooping. It was as if his
neck could not sustain what his eyes and face wanted to do. 'What's
going on out there?' he asked. I told him there was nothing to
worry about. Betty washed up and went outside. My father and I
spent the first part of the evening like all the others, in the sitting
room. It was as hot an evening as every other; and, in our suburban
street, as quiet. The sodium lamps outside had only themselves for
company. The white-painted, wooden gate at the end of the garden

path hung slightly askew, as it always had. Then we went to bed, quite early.

My room was the one I had slept in as a child. I could hear furtive comings and goings taking place in the back yard, just a few yards away from my wide open sash window, in its delapidated wooden frame. For a long time I resisted the temptation to look out. Then there were sounds of grapplings, slaps, the back gate slamming. Loud laughter. Song. Exchanges in Xhosa or Sesuto, of which I could not understand a word. More bird-cries and arguments. When I finally looked out, I heard suddenly, from every quarter of the moonlit, lamplit horizon, darkened only by the shapes of trees and houses, the hooting of car horns and distant voices. It was midnight. The New Year had begun. I went back to bed. Rebecca thrust her head through my window. The air was filled instantly with the smell of Cape sherry. She was wearing not much clothing; no more than a petticoat, as far as I could make out. 'Heppy-heppy, master!' she cried. 'It's Heppy New Year!' Out of the darkness, prone on my bed, I solemnly wished her a happy New Year. Then I told her to make less noise. Her head withdrew. The smell of sherry lingered. Minutes later she was sitting directly under my window, on the verandah, sobbing industriously and resisting the drunken attempts of Betty and friends to move her away. She was crying, it seemed, because I had been 'too cross' with her.

At that point I really did become cross. By about two in the morning all was silent. Betty was back in her room. The guests had departed. Rebecca, still wearing only her petticoat, had wandered out of the back gate, headed in no particular direction or towards no particular destination. I did not care. She returned some time during the next afternoon. Betty was too hungover to do any work. The cooking was in my hands once again. My father had heard nothing of it all. He did not even know it was New Year's day, and complained bitterly because the daily newspaper did not arrive as usual.

For my farewell dinner a week later Betty made a big effort. My train to Johannesburg, from where I would take the plane to

London, was due to leave at ten in the evening, and a taxi had been ordered to come and pick me up well in advance. For the first time during my stay, my father and I ate not in the breakfast room at the back of the house; but in state, so to speak, in the dining room, surrounded by the heavy mahogany furniture of late-Victorian vintage which had been in the house when my parents had purchased it forty years before. The table, the chairs, the sideboards (one of them equipped with a mirror and overarching pediment six or eight feet wide) abounded in fluted legs and befoliated capitals; they broke out in roses on every possible surface; the wood was as gleaming and ruddy as something seen by the light of a coal fire. Betty waited on us in her smartest white uniform, a white cap on her head. Rebecca too had dolled herself up for the occasion. Once again the best napery, cutlery, and china had been put out. Four courses came and went. The effect was overpoweringly funereal.

Yet the most emphatic and unexpected indication of the specialness of the evening was still to come. Once we had finished eating, Betty disappeared. Rebecca was left to do the clearing and washing up. My father and I went to the sitting room. About ten minutes later Betty reappeared. She had divested herself of her best garb as a servant and had put on her best dress as a woman. It was a floral print, rather gauzy in effect, with an elaborate, frilled neck. She had also changed her cap. Now that she was arrayed like a guest, she treated herself as one. She sat in the room with us, which she had not done at any time during my stay, and joined in our talk. Most of it was about absent members of the family. Betty herself was childless and – though she had had many male friends, some of whom had kept her company for years at a stretch – husbandless. Thus she had no family other than the one for which she had worked for the previous two decades and more. She knew everything about us and our children – birthdays, examination results, jobs, tastes in food. She spoke of all of us generously and affectionately; it would have been inconceivable for her to do otherwise on this occasion. My father listened, commented, got muddled up among his grandchildren, got bored, started fiddling with his radio and succeeded in producing sufficient noise from it to prevent the conversation continuing. So Betty and I sat together without exchanging any further reminiscences or speculations about the future.

The noise from the radio was not loud enough to prevent us hearing the sound of a car door slamming in the street outside, and footsteps coming up the garden path. It was time to go. The desolation of departure seemed to be limitless in scope and yet confined to a single, crowded, overtaxed place in my breast. There was also, as there so often is, a certain sense of relief to it. The thing had to be done. Then let it be done. Rebecca, as insouciant as a cat, and as curious, had come from the back of the house to lend a hand with the suitcases and to join in the leavetaking. Betty was in tears; my father almost so. He insisted on accompanying me to the gate. We exchanged only a few words. Once I and my bags had been installed in the taxi, I saw that he and Betty had already turned in the shadow and light of the path, and were making their way back along it, towards the steps that led to the verandah and so to the open door of the house. He was leaning heavily on her arm; their progress could hardly have been slower. Then the car started. Every house we passed, at first, was as familiar to me as the camber of the road itself.

Strangely enough, it was not my father but Betty whom I was never to see again. She did indeed stay with him 'to the end' as she had promised me she would: to her end. Nothing had been further from our thoughts, when she had used that phrase in conversation with me, than that things would turn out that way. Within about twelve months of my visit she died of a heart attack. At that point my father finally succumbed to the urgings of my oldest brother, and went to live in his house in Johannesburg. He survived Betty for little more than three years. Throughout that time, first month by month, then week by week, then day by day, he became more and more frail physically, and more and more clouded and distracted in mind.

PATIENT

I

pancreas: a broad strip of glandular tissue across the back of the abdomen, mostly under the cover of the stomach. It is broadest on the right where it nestles round the portal vein and is closely applied to the arteries of the liver and the bile duct.

pancreatitis: inflamation of the pancreas – may be mild and transient, but at its worst can be very dangerous with a clinical picture suggesting either severe disease of the gall bladder or perforation of a duodenal ulcer.

The Penguin Medical Dictionary

The house surgeon was a blond, tender-skinned young woman, with irises of so pale a blue, set in such wide, weary whites, they looked almost grey. Her hair was drawn back, but wisps of it escaped at her temples and forehead, and formed a kind of soft, irregular frame for her face. It gave a certain pathos to the earnestness of her expression. Fatigue had flattened the skin against her cheek-bones and left bruises under her eyes; her voice sounded effortful and distant. She told me she had been up all night. Now, at 7.30 a.m., there I lay, in a cubicle just off the casualty ward, having been turned out of the ambulance on to a high, hard, wheeled stretcher. More work.

It was thirty-five years since I had last been a patient in a hospital. I had been admitted then after a car accident. This admission seemed to me almost as revolutionary or cataclysmic as the last. More than twelve hours before, at a meeting, I had begun to feel pain across my stomach and the lower part of my chest; severe enough pain to make for a bizarre discontinuity between the voices of the committee members, my inner preoccupations, and what I hoped was my wholly unrevealing demeanour. As for what followed: perhaps I can best convey the feeling of it by saying that during the small hours of the morning I became convinced that a cruelly sensitive cord or organ which should have lain horizontally somewhere in my chest had become twisted into a figure of eight, and that if only I knew how, possibly if I retched violently enough, I would be able to flip it back into position, and make it lie flat again. Then the pain and sickness would stop and I would be able to sleep.

Well, the trick was beyond me. Everything was beyond me: control, escape, comprehension. Nevertheless, when my wife did finally rouse a doctor from his bed to come to mine, towards dawn, I felt a kind of perverse relief at seeing how alarmed he was by my condition. At least I wasn't making a fuss about nothing! The ambulance he summoned came after a brief delay. Wrapped in the traditional red blanket I was carried downstairs swiftly and with great deftness. It was too early in the morning for any of the neighbours to be looking on, which was something to be grateful for. On the way to the hospital, in the throbbing room-like interior of the vehicle, the man sitting with me asked what I did for a living. I told him I taught English at a college. 'Oh, then I better speak proper,' he said, sitting up smartly, with a mock attempt at an upper-class accent.

The next four days and nights passed in disorderly fashion. They left intense but fitful memories. The impossibility (because of a familiar pain) of continuing to lie on my left side; and the impossibility (because of the fear of a new pain) of turning over on my right. Waking at some unknown hour to find a West Indian staff nurse standing at the bedside, gazing down at me, and hearing her whisper, 'I frightened you.' My wish to tell her that nothing could have been further from the truth – how could I have been frightened by so intent and concerned a presence as the first thing

I was conscious of? – and my utter inability to bring out a single word of this complicated thought. A corner of sullenly clouded sky hanging between straining concrete beams. Its sullenness turning to grimness as each day wore on. The intolerable smell of food at mealtimes in the ward. The smell of rain, brought in on the hair and shoulders of visitors, though not a drop of it could be seen on the windows. Getting to know by sight, by the touch of my free hand, by the touch of my tongue, by the weight and heat of it at all hours, the plastic splint on which my arm with the drip-needle in it was bound. Time passing, at night especially, even more slowly than on a long plane flight (and hardly less noisily, because of the roar of the air-conditioning vents in the ceiling), so that a thirty-minute leap of the hands of the watch was a victory, something achieved against the odds, which brought nearer land-fall or daybreak. Spells of sleep induced by yellow, ovoid pills, each spell ending with the convulsive sensation of being flung backwards into waking, as if into a wall. The dehydration of my lips and tongue, and the sense of their growing bigger and bigger with every hour that passed. A day of high fever during which I had no control whatever over the verbose, boring madman in my skull, who endlessly lectured me in pompously editorialising fashion on subjects I know nothing about: Britain's relations with the Common Market, the industrialisation of Tsarist Russia (complete with nonsensical map), the history of the alphabet.

Still, some time during the third or fourth day the sign reading 'Nil by Mouth' above the bed was replaced by one that said 'Clear Fluids Only'. I found myself able to turn over without having to steel myself to it beforehand. My blood pressure was no longer being measured so frequently; nervous medical students came less often to take blood samples from my inner arm. ('Don't let sister see I've spilled some blood on the sheet,' one of them said, hastily covering up the tell-tale blobs with the blanket. 'I was afraid you'd be an old woman with fallen veins,' said another.) The fever withdrew or shrank to a single seed of darkness in the pit of my brain. The drip was put on a mobile stand, and I was encouraged to hobble about the ward, rolling my life-support system with me, like an astronaut on the moon. I was able to stand by the window at nightfall, looking at a bank of dark, bruised red in the west, under which the buildings of London lay in black heaps: all of which had an extraordinary resemblance to coals in a grate casting their glow above them.

By this time I had registered the other people in the room as rather more than vague presences. There was Mr C, whose ragged but elaborately orchestrated snores were such a torment to me. There was bantam-cock Mr B ('in fashion') and his greying coiffure, stiff with grease, who had undergone exploratory surgery and was now desperately anxious to learn – and not to learn – the results of a biopsy. There was Mr G, another more subdued or philosophical attender on a biopsy result, whose fur-bedecked and perfumed wife chirped and clucked at him in cosy-sounding Polish every evening. There was the nameless, elderly Portuguese who suffered from a urinary complaint, and who would sit all day in an armchair, with an array of disposable 'bottles' on a table in front of him; these he was always shuffling and re-arranging like chess-men, every now and again surreptitiously burying one under the blankets in his lap and then returning it to its place in the parade above. He apparently had no English at all; from time to time the nurses would try to communicate with him by getting one of the Filipino cleaning women, of whom there appeared to be scores, to shout unsuccessfully at him in Spanish.

Some of the nurses I had got to know by name (Sarah, Pene-lope); to some I gave names of my own (Princess Anne, the Asian Flu); most of them remained as anonymous to me as I was to them. At times I was conscious of being the object of their professional concern, and occasionally, of something stranger, their profes-sional tenderness. Only at the rarest moments, however, was any recognition of my individuality reflected back to me from their regard.

Their scrutinising yet indifferent gaze was just another manifes-tation of the change that had been brought about by illness, of the self-severing transition I had gone through. But for me or any other patient to complain of the 'impersonality' of the treatment we received in that hospital would be almost as much beside the point as for a customer to feel aggrieved because a car he buys in a showroom is not manufactured especially for him. A high degree of impersonality was not an incidental drawback of the treatment offered there; it was its very condition, that without which it could neither have been conceived nor administered. This was not only a function of the size of the hospital and the rapidity of its turnover of patients. Nor was it only a consequence of the ever-renewed yet never-wholly-sufficient disciplinary effort that was needed to sustain the routines of the place – cleaning, feeding, record-keeping, bed-making, and the rest – which could take no account of the wants or feelings of any one patient at any particular moment. Even beyond all these was the impersonality of the medical technology which the system had both developed and been shaped by. If the young houseman who had admitted me and her senior registrar were able to tell me, even before I had left the casualty ward, that I was suffering from a severe attack of pancreatitis, this was not because of their knowledge of my individual history, or because they possessed some intuitive, diagnostic skill which had led them to the truth. It was because a numbered sample of my blood had been sent for urgent analysis to the appropriate department of the hospital; within thirty minutes the machines and computers there had (fortunately for me) made certain unequivocal readings which had been sent back to the casualty ward. The doctors had then known how to proceed; in the short run, at any rate. That both of them had spoken sympathetically and reassuringly on my arrival had meant a great deal to me; but even their self-assurance was in large part derived from the fact that they knew they were parts of a system much larger than themselves.

However, the system did have a haphazard workhouse or almshouse side to its activities whose existence I would never have suspected beforehand. Subsequent, or consequential, periods in the hospital were to make this even plainer to me. On this occasion, for bureaucratic reasons which were never explained (I was left uneasily to think up my own reasons for the change) I was suddenly transferred on the fourth day of my stay from the ward I had been in to another three storeys higher. The room I was put in this time contained two long-stay patients – residents, rather – who were always wandering around; the ward as a whole was untidier and seemed to be run in a more disorganised fashion than the last, perhaps because it was almost wholly staffed by free-lance nurses from various agencies, whose attachment to the hospital, its routines, and their own duties seemed looser than those in the ward below. But it was the presence of Roger and John (as I shall call them), the two residents mentioned above, which accounted for most of the noise and disorder in the room itself. They also introduced into the ward a kind of grim hospital comedy that was inseparable from the pathos of the position they were in.

Roger, a man in his mid-fifties, had had a stroke many months before; like other permanent inhabitants of the hospital whom I was to come across during the further spells I was shortly to spend in it, he was kept in the ward simply because there was nowhere else for him to go. He must have been an imposing man once. He was tall and portly, with a protruding jaw and a fleshy nose to match; he had a deep voice and a positively lordly accent. None of these advantages was of any use to him now. He walked with two sticks, goose-stepping with one foot and dragging the other, while leaning backward at an angle of about fifteen or twenty degrees from the vertical. He spent some of his time sitting in a throne-like chair at one end of the room, from which he could watch everything that was going on; he also used to station himself next to the sister's desk at the centre of the ward, again with an expression of deep, inspectorial attentiveness to what was passing before him. Every now and again, however, he would take off, and then there would be a noisy but unalarmed flap among the nurses. 'Where's Roger?' one would hear them cry. 'What's happened to Roger?' Then they would find him in one of the adjacent wards, or in the

foyer outside (weeks later I was to see him scrutinising the proceedings in a ward many floors below the one he inhabited), and
they would ceremoniously escort him back to his room, with a
different set of cries and giggles. 'You are a naughty boy, Roger.
What do you think you're up to?' and so forth.

They washed him, they shaved him, they helped him to eat, and
once, when he seized hold of the bottom of one of his escorts, they
smacked him, squealing with excitement at this unexpected sign of
life. For the most part Roger remained silent, the creaking of his
walk back and forth excepted; but occasionally he made kindly,
patronising remarks to the people around him. 'You carry on,' he
told me once, when I looked up from doing nothing at all on his
entry into the room; and then, as if to palliate any impression of
discourtesy this instruction might have made: 'I have some work
to do.' The voice and manner were perfect. He spoke with such
conviction an eavesdropper could never have known how utterly
without substance was what he had just said. Another time he asked
me if I had met his sister when she had 'paid a call'. I said no. 'Pity,'
he said. 'You would have enjoyed her company.'

Sullen, moustached, long-haired John, thirty or more years
younger than Roger, came from the other end of the social scale.
Whatever his family did, however, they had earned enough out of
it to equip their ailing son with bowls of the most expensive-
looking fruit, numerous bottles of different kinds of soft drink, a
three-deck cassette tape-player, and a portable television set which
was parked on a table next to his bed. These last two he played
loudly and alternately until I asked a nurse to tell him to turn them
down. She received the request ill-humouredly, but did what I
asked; with even greater ill-humour John then donned a pair of
earphones. The sound still leaked through, but it was not nearly as
overpowering as before. He invariably wore a pair of hospital-
issue pyjamas and a polka-dotted, maroon dressing-gown. The
garments were shed for his wash morning and evening, and the
body then revealed was mole-spotted and unmuscled. But one
would not have known anything was wrong with him had his

stomach not been supported by some kind of girdle of whitish panels and pink, elasticated straps.

He had been in the hospital for three months or more, I gathered, waiting to have an operation for what he described as 'water on the stomach'. Though 'bed rest' (and a salt-free diet) had been ordered for him, he would never spend more than half-an-hour on his bed during the day without getting up and darting off on some forlorn, self-invented errand: to the shop on the ground floor, from which he would come back laden with an assortment of comestibles; to visit people in the other wards; to have a smoke in the 'day-room', where another, larger television set boomed and roared away at all hours. He also had a kind of girl friend, who was herself a patient, apparently, but who was not even obliged, as he was, to wear pyjamas. Instead she wore tight jeans, a tight sweater, a ribbon in her dyed hair, and plenty of lipstick. She was always coming and going, sometimes accompanied by her acolyte: yet another fully clothed demi-patient, a boy of about fourteen, who seemed to go about in a trance of pride at the adult company he was keeping. The three of them frequently went into a huddle around John's bed before starting up in search of some excitement.

The biggest excitement of all during my stay in the room was the great take-away curry scandal. On what turned out to be (for the time being, anyway) my last night in the hospital, John came in with his girlfriend at about 10 p.m. This was after I had swallowed the more or less obligatory sleeping pills which were distributed every night. He and she whispered together for a while; then the girl left. In the half-darkened room John proceeded to take out of his locker some underclothes, a sweater adorned with the motto and coat of arms of the University of Chicago, a pair of jeans and a pair of sneakers. He put these on hastily, with an air of great furtiveness. At the door he scanned the corridor to the right and left, before slipping away. Hours later I was conscious of his returning, undressing, and getting into bed. By morning it was clear that trouble was afoot. The nurses who woke us up did so without cheery words. To John they did not speak at all. He lay on his bed with his head under the pillow. This did not stop the Filipino girl who wheeled in the tea-trolley from yelling at him, 'Wait until sister come!' – to which John responded with a writhe that sent his head yet deeper under the pillow. When the sister did finally come, she glanced perfunctorily around the room at the rest of us, before advancing on John's bed. She pulled the pillow away from his ear, and, jabbing her finger at him with each phrase, pronounced her sentence: 'You are not to get out of this bed, you are not even to go to the toilet, a bottle and a bed-pan will be given to you, the curtain will be drawn, and you will stay behind it until doctor comes.'

The curtains were drawn around John's bed, and she left the room. Dead silence. Roger, who had already taken up his position on his throne, gazed at the shrouded corner of the room with his steadfast, bewildered stare. The man in the bed nearest to me, a bespectacled sufferer from gall-bladder disease, shrugged and I did likewise. Presently the canteen staff proffered John his breakfast through the curtains. It was refused with a single yelp. Silence again. At last the senior registrar came on her round. She was a tall, small-faced, olive-complexioned woman, with dark hair severely cropped and (usually) a rather frank and thoughtful manner. On this particular morning she revealed a feline streak to her character. When the curtains around his bed were drawn back, and the full length of John was once again revealed to view, she approached him quietly. 'Well, John,' she asked, 'did you enjoy your take-away curry last night?'

She waited a long time for an answer. None was forthcoming. So, eventually, she assumed one. 'No? What a pity, when you went to so much trouble to get it.'

After another long silence, during which John stared motionlessly up at her and she stared down at him, she changed her tack abruptly. 'You're a waste of time,' she told him. 'You're a waste of money. You're a waste of our patience. You're not worth bothering about. We keep you here because we want to make you better, we put you on a strict, salt-free diet, and what do you do? – you run out at night to the nearest curry house!'

'I just had chicken and chips,' John interjected pathetically.

The remark was ignored. 'So what do you want us to do with you? Kick you out? Restrain you physically? You try one more trick like that, and not only will we not do the operation on you, I'll see to it that you're never let into this hospital again. Is that clear?' There was no answer from John. So she repeated the question, and repeated it yet again, until he finally answered in a muffled voice, yes it was clear. 'Right. Now you lie on that bed until I give you permission to get up from it.'

Whereupon she left the room. Two nurses remained behind and swathed John in a white blanket: not physically restraining him in the sense that he could not have undone their work, but nevertheless making as good a job as they could of turning him into a mummy. John lay passively on his back throughout this process. Once the nurses had left the room he began cursing at the ceiling. 'Fucking doctor. Fucking nurses. Fucking hospital. Fucking doctor . . .' The litany went on for a while; then he started crying.

He was still wrapped up, but silently so, by the time I left the hospital a few hours later. I was supposed to have stayed there for another couple of days before going through the first of a series of tests intended to establish the underlying cause of the attack. (It subsequently became clear that I too had been suffering, without knowing it, from gall-bladder disease; but for various reasons it was only on my fourth admission to the hospital that the offending organ was finally plucked out.) Once the idea of getting out of the place for the next two days had occurred to me, I could not rest until I had secured the doctors' agreement to it. Thus my ejection from the hospital on this occasion had something of the suddenness of my entry into it. The last person I spoke to was John's girlfriend, who came running up to me in the foyer on the ground floor, in the hope that I would tell her everything that had happened that morning. She knew and I knew that she was the one who had put him up to the curry house escapade; she even told me that the hospital staff had seen the pair of them leaving the curry house.

And now? Scared and thrilled, she wanted to know above all if I was going to tell tales and get her into trouble too.

On that boarding-school note I was out of the building and travelling across the Heath on an ordinary, wanly sunlit autumn morning. There were few cars about. Overcoated people sat on benches or walked at a sedate pace on the pavements. The un-treated air was so cool, I felt I should sip at it rather than simply breathe it in. Everything my eye fell on looked astonishingly frail and random: leaves hanging on by their very fingertips to the twigs above them; trees in purple, russet and yellow masses, each wrapped in a faint mist, as a sleeping man might be wrapped in his own breath; subdued, defenceless stretches of trodden grass. After the flat rectilinearity of the surfaces in the hospital, it was impossible not to be overwhelmed by the irregularity and profusion of the autumnal growth visible everywhere: the infinite gradations of its colour, the variety of its textures, its sideways saggings and downwards flutterings, its upward strivings and spreadings. Yet how provisional it all appeared to be; how uncertain the hold that any of it had on itself.

II

Dippy-dippy-dation, my operation:
How many stitches did you have?

Children's Counting Song

Six weeks after first being taken to the hospital, and with two investigatory sojourns between, I returned there to have my gall-bladder removed. This is of course a positively banal or routine surgical procedure (routine for the surgeons, that is, not for the patients); indeed, a timely newspaper article had informed me that it was the 'major surgical intervention most commonly carried out in Great Britain'. I had been told that the operation would prevent a recurrence of attacks of pancreatitis like the one I had been through: a promise or invitation I was not disposed to reject.

So there I was, admitted once again to that foreign country which is never more than a few minutes or miles away from any of us. The operation was still a full two-and-a-half days off. In the bed alongside mine was a geriatric patient named Teddy. I did not know, and still do not know, why I was admitted so early: apparently that was the standard procedure. For Teddy there was no going back and forth, no crossing of frontiers, no letters or visitors from that remote kingdom which began just outside the hospital doors. His entire life was spent either on his bed or in a wheel chair. In the mornings the nurses unplugged his catheter and its receptacle; then they took him to the bathroom; then they propped him up in a chair, in his pyjamas and dressing gown, with a blanket over his knees. They never failed to put his checked cloth cap on his head; occasionally, for a laugh, they put it on back to front. Thus adorned, he sat through the day: sometimes sleeping, sometimes staring, sometimes shouting (if he managed to catch anyone's eye), 'Hoy! Hoy!' or 'How about it, then?' When he opened his mouth three long green teeth showed. 'Where's me sandwiches?' was another favourite cry. The young men in the ward responded to it by giving him bananas and biscuits from their private store; when they gave him a cigarette he promptly began to eat that, too.

Shortly after the cigarette-eating incident I was moved out of Teddy's room into a specially made-up bed in the 'high dependency' section of the ward. This was directly in front of the table where the nurses sat and did their paper work; it was separated from them only by a low parapet, so that they could see at a glance whether any of the patients needed their attention. Items of emergency and resuscitatory equipment were also kept there, affixed to the walls. At last, after hanging about for two days in a state of useless anticipation, enlivened only by repeated form-filling and examinations by every grade of medical staff and student in the hierarchy, I had been brought up into the front-line. Or so I thought. Naturally I was depressed and anxious about what lay ahead, as well as impatient to get to it, to have the next night and morning over. Then I would go into a gulf, an abyss, a place of darkness which was unknowable by definition, and from which I would emerge like another of the bloodless, prostrate, unconscious, white-swathed creatures whom I had seen being wheeled into the ward from the operating theatre. How could one imagine oneself becoming like one of them? How could one not try to do so?

In the pre-dawn darkness, the grim, Aztec-like rituals of preparation began. A breakfast of corn-flakes and tea with milk was given to me (this because I was due to go into the theatre only in the mid-afternoon); I bathed in water treated with a special iodoform mixture; my stomach was shaved; a suppository was administered; I donned white, sacrificial garments – a brief nightgown with tapes that tied at the back, a chef's hat, little cloth slippers. Just how anxious I was, in going through these procedures, became apparent to me when I noticed that I had begun to treat my body with a special solicitude, as if it already had some deep injury inflicted on it, whereas the truth was that nothing at all had happened; I was quite as capable of walking out of the hospital as I had been of walking into it, two days before.

Instead I lay in bed in my white nightgown, trying without much success to read a book, or listening as if across a great space to the casual conversation of the nurses on the other side of the parapet, or to the monologue of one of the other patients in the section. The talker was an elderly, elongated man, with exceptionally large feet and hands, whose presence in that room was something of a mystery, since he was well enough to be discharged directly from it, on that very day, into the great world outside. Some of the things he said were rather mysterious too. For instance, he firmly told the huddled, silent heaps of bed-clothes who were his only auditors, 'As far as I'm concerned the Edgware Road is the road north out of London' – as if any of us had been arguing that it ran south out of London. Some birds flying past the seventh-floor window produced another authoritative ruling from him:

'They must be rooks, since crows don't fly that high.'

The hours seemed to go by even more slowly than they had the previous night. Before a patient was taken down to the theatre, I had been told, a 'pre-med' was administered, to make him drowsy. Then the preparations would be complete, and darkness would supervene. When the staff-nurse finally approached me, well after midday, I sat up almost eagerly, to take my medicine like a man. Or rather, like a child. At that point there took place the only 'mishap' I have to report, as far as my own treatment is concerned. The nurse had not come to give me my 'pre-med'; far from it. She had come to tell me that I would not, after all, be operated on that afternoon; indeed, the operation would not take place until the next Monday. (It was then Thursday.) They had miscalculated the time needed in the theatre by the two patients who had preceded me there.

All that apprehension for nothing? All of it to go through again? These last days of strenuous waiting, and these last hours of pre- paration, utterly without point? The shock of that announcement was in its own way quite as painful as anything I had felt since I had fallen ill; in some respects it was even worse than any of the other pains I had suffered or was still to go through, for it had not come about through an act of nature, as it were, but as a result of human misjudgement and mismanagement. Anger, incredulity, paranoid suspicion (I *knew*, I'd always known, they were capable of pulling something like this on me; I'd always known *I'd* be the one they would do it to), shame, impotence, even a tiny, sneaking flicker of relief – it does not take long, no more than a second it seems, for such conflicting and mutually exacerbating emotions to fill one's breast. To get them to settle down is a more protracted business.

In the end, however, the torment-by-anti-climax I had been put through did produce two incidental benefits. The first was that the wintry weekend I found myself unexpectedly spending at home (two long black nights and three brown days, accompanied throughout by the sound of leaves creeping and crackling in the streets) turned out to be surprisingly enjoyable. The second was that when I did return to the hospital on Sunday, to be prepared all over again for the operation, I felt none of the apprehension I had gone through on the previous occasion. I did not give a damn about anything but getting the whole performance over and done with; I certainly was not going to let them make a fool of me again by investing emotion in it beforehand.

So: into the gulf. Its antechamber was a bare, disorderly-seeming room, with a high ceiling and many parked trolleys to one side; it echoed with clashing noises whose origin I could not determine. For some reason the room reminded me of a large greenhouse or conservatory. In that place, amid those noises, recollection comes to a stop. The anaesthetic was not administered there, I am sure; but I have no memory of anything that followed, until I found myself in the ward, on my back, hung about with, indeed penetrated by, drips and drains and aspirators. It was morning. My throat ached.

Had I slept right through the evening and night, after the operation? It seemed to me that I had. Some time later, however, my wife asked if I did not remember seeing her when I had first been brought back from the recovery room. Then, at once, I did recall seeing her; I remembered the distant, troubled smile on her face, which seemed to rise out of an ocean-like turmoil or heaving going on all around her. That this was a genuine memory, and not merely a response to her suggestion, I know by the fact that in the same moment I remembered something she had not told me: namely, that I had been looking at her over a set of bars which had been put up around my bed. I could even remember the feeling of bitterness and dismay which this bit of apparatus had produced. The last time I had seen such bars they had been around Teddy's bed. 'So that's what they think of me!' I'd protested inwardly.

Over the next two days I flopped and floundered through a welter of discomfort and weakness as if through an endless, bottomless bog which was, bewilderingly enough, my own body. Nothing *worked*; nothing could be relied on; whatever was not felt as an intolerable pressure of one kind or another made itself known as an even more alarming absence. Of direct pain, however, I felt remarkably little; indeed, as long as I lay perfectly still I suffered no pain at all. But how could that be managed for more than a few minutes at a time? Every cough, every hiccup, tore through the whole mess like a bullet. Every movement was a reminder of what I would have been going through had it not been for the pain-killing drugs which, in solution with the saline drip above the bed, were constantly being piped into me.

Those drugs, presumably, also piped into me the hallucinations I kept on having or being visited by. They were strangely colour-less, plotless, pointless affairs, for all their more-than-dreamlike insistence. Against a background that was as grey and lustreless as they themselves were, there gathered above me diaphonous, quasi-human figures who whispered and chirped and clutched me tightly by the wrist or arm or shoulder. Usually it was by their grip on me, in the first instance, that I would know them to be back, each time. Of human shape, they were without human faces; of human size, they had no more substance than an insect's wing. But they did have exceptionally firm fingers. They could stare too, their facelessness notwithstanding. To be conscious that they were not really there, to know that I was awake, that when I looked for them I could see nothing, was never enough to drive them away. A moment later they would return – staring, shuffling, gripping, exchanging the dry crepitations that passed for speech in their washed-out, twilight world. Dreams would have had incompar-ably greater emotional affect than these visitations; dreams would also have had far more colour and narrative substance. But the phantoms were still at it, days later; once they even got their fingers right inside my jaw, in order to force my head back and hold it there, for what seemed to be a long, long time. Subsequently it occurred to me that these creatures and the activities they went in for might have been some kind of 'after-image' of the operation itself, when I had certainly been surrounded by masked, firm-fingered attendants; but that is nothing more than a guess, an attempt to make sense of what otherwise would appear to have been wholly senseless.

On the third day after the operation I was moved from the high dependency section to one of the four-bedded rooms into which the rest of the ward was divided. Evidently my recovery up to that stage had been satisfactory; and so it continued to be. In ways that actually seemed to be more mysterious than the pain and discomfort I was going through, an increase of strength came to me, or I came to it, day by day, sometimes even hour by hour, in unpredictable accessions. You feel illness, moment by moment; it is something you are conscious of; your consciousness is the sure sign that you are ill. Recovery, on the other hand, comes by stealth. Each stage precedes your realising that you have passed it. Every day, however short of breath I still was, and however hobbled my step was by that crushed, post-operative crouch which marked off the veterans from the apprehensive newcomers, who now stared at me just as I had stared at my predecessors on my arrival, I could walk a little further; every night I could stretch my legs a little straighter in the bed; eating, drinking and evacuation (the last after a wretched delay) became somewhat less of an ordeal.

Curiously enough, this progress did not appear to be retarded by the depression which accompanied it, and which grew stronger, if anything, as I grew stronger physically. It took the form initially of a sense of failure which referred not just to my ailing body, but to myself, to my life, to everything I had ever done or tried to do. It was not that I felt myself to be a failure, because I was there; rather, the truth seemed to be that I was there because I was a failure. The episode, which had begun about six weeks before, could not be seen, in other words, as an intrusion in my life or an interruption of it; it was its epitome, an essential expression of it. This conviction somehow appeared to be certified by or objectified in the flat, pinkish, four-square walls of the room, in its beige, rubberised floor-covering, in the plastic venetian blinds over its windows, in the honeycomb light fixture which threw a fluorescent glare into every crevice of the room, or, after lights-out, kept a small blue worm suspended in its grip all night through.

That same conviction of failure took another form when I caught a glimpse of myself in a mirror while having my first bath (itself a milestone on the way to recovery). What I saw there was not my face but my father's, in the last few years of his life; and not just his face but the attentive, listening tilt of his head, the wariness of the movements of his eyes, the habitual expression of unhappiness on his features. So far from those modes of his selfhood having vanished into the grave with him, as I had imagined, I had incorporated and re-created them within myself. Now the moment had come for them to make themselves manifest.

Whatever mental miseries the others in the room were going through, they were not, as they were in my case, those accompanying the process of recovery. I say that for the starkest of reasons. The others in the room were not recovering. They were dying, all three of them. In the bed across from me there lay a tall, emaciated man, somewhat younger than myself, whom I shall call Harry: he was a terminal cancer patient. In the bed on my right was old Mr K, a diabetic with high blood pressure, who was slowly drifting away, like an unmoored boat, into silence and darkness, with only an occasional Yiddish-inflected exclamation of bemused greeting or enquiry to let one know how far he had gone or had still to go. And in the bed diagonally across from me was Mr F, another elderly man, whose demeanour compared with the others was quite alert and whose complexion was positively rubicund. However, one Friday lunch-time, when the house-officer going off duty bade him farewell with a hearty, 'See you on Monday,' Mr F replied firmly, 'I hope you won't.' 'Don't be *silly*!' the house-officer brayed at him, in such resonantly public-school tones the words seemed to clatter off the walls like tin cans. 'What a *silly* thing to say!'

Later that afternoon Mr F had visitors: his wife, who was herself in a wheel chair, and his jerky, tweed-suited, spinster daughter of middle-age. They were fussing about him with their gifts of fruit, flowers, and Perrier water, when he began to groan heavily and to roll about on the bed; a moment later, still groaning, he was on his back and slowly but irresistibly arching his whole body upwards, higher and higher, until it was braced like a bridge between his shoulders and his heels. One could not have believed it possible for so old and plump a man to remain suspended like that, but he managed it. Then he collapsed. Almost immediately, with yet another groan – and somehow the sight was even harder to believe this time than the last – he had begun to arch himself upwards yet again. His wife was frantically wheeling her chair back and forth; the daughter pressed the buzzer, abandoned it, and ran into the corridor for help; both of them were uttering incoherent cries. A nurse came in and the curtains were drawn around the bed. From behind them came more groans, some loud, some like whispers, as well as the voices of mother and daughter pathetically crying, 'Relax! Just relax!' as if the man were being fractious or bringing his sufferings on himself. Finally the relief houseman arrived, on the run. The curtains were drawn back only after Mr F had been rendered senseless with a shot of morphine.

The houseman, a neatly combed, good-looking, kind-hearted boy in his early twenties, then had to deal with the wife and daughter. This he did by telling them that Doctor This and Doctor That would be coming to see the patient as soon as they possibly could; they would be out of the theatre at 5 p.m. and they would then attend to him immediately. So the two women started to wait for the arrival of the doctors. They could be heard in the corridors uttering to one another the doctors' names, the houseman's included, like talismans; as five o'clock approached they began to ask every passing nurse when the doctors would be coming; Mrs F could be heard talking on the pay-phone, with a kind of reverential despair, of their imminent arrival, as if of the coming of some wonder-working, all-knowing creatures belonging to another race.

At about 7.00 p.m. a whole team of these doctor-saviours did finally appear. 'Sod it!' I heard the central one among them exclaiming to his colleagues, as they stood in a group in the corridor. 'The

old bastard's gone and blocked himself. We'll have to operate
tonight . . .' He was, needless to say, well out of earshot of Mrs
and Miss F. There was not only irritation in his voice but also a
kind of battlefield exhilaration at the thought of the fatigue and
effort that lay ahead, and of his own capacity to do whatever might
be demanded of him. Shortly afterwards Mr F was wheeled out
of the room. The next morning he could be seen in the high-
dependency section, with more than the usual amounts of para-
phenalia hanging over him, and an oxygen mask affixed to his
paper-coloured face. Later that morning I bumped into mother and
daughter in the corridor: the younger woman's expression was
worn and red-eyed and quite without hope; the mother's face
looked half the size it had been the previous day. Her eyes sought
mine from below, from the wheel-chair, with a mixture of shame
and mute appeal, as if I too might yet miraculously turn into a
source of help. Later still, Mr F's son arrived, with *his* adolescent
son in tow: the man stood at the foot of his father's bed, mopping
his eyes and face with a handkerchief; the boy simply gazed with
incredulity and fascination at his slumped yet strung-up grandfather. By the time I left hospital, three days on, thirteen days after
entering the room Teddy lived in, Mr F had not recovered
consciousness.

Within an hour of his departure from the room, Mr L was
wheeled into it. He was in pretty good shape; quite evidently well
on the way to recovering from the hernia operation he had been
through. He and I used to go on hobbling patrols together, up and
down the corridors of the ward. I did not tell him what had happened to his predecessor in the corner of the room he now occupied, and nor did either of the others: Mr K because he almost
certainly did not know; Harry, the cancer patient, because he did
not care. He had enough woes of his own.

It was his wife – an Irish woman with dyed, silver-blonde hair
permed into ripples exactly like sea sand after the tide had with-
drawn – who told me that he was a terminal case. She had also said
that he did not know it. But I think he did. The more I saw of him

the more convinced I became that he had no expectation of ever getting out of the place. One of the ways in which this showed, strangely enough, was in the sweetness of his behaviour to the nurses, compared to the harshness with which he treated his wife. Nothing she did pleased him: not the food or newspapers or changes of pyjamas she brought him, or the length of her visits, or the subjects she chose to speak about. For her he had snarls and curses ('stupid bitch', 'silly cow'); for the nurses, on whom he was now dependent during all the hours she was away, he had only humble beseechings and coos of thanks. At regular intervals he received quantities of sedatives and painkillers: small, red capsules which clattered in the plastic container in which they were given to him, orange and yellow syrups with a powerful smell, the occasional shot from a hypodermic needle. These enabled him to drowse some of the hours away, either lying on his bed or sitting in an armchair. When he was awake he never looked out of the window, read a newspaper, went to the day room to watch television, or listened to the radio through the headphones hanging above each bed. He had given them up, together with the world outside which they represented.

In the evenings, after the nurse had made up his bed for the night, he always lay on top of the bedclothes, his feet presented to mine. The evening *cafard* would settle down on the ward. Nothing to do now until some kind of unconsciousness would intervene at an uncertain hour of the night. Nothing to look forward to but the arrival of the drugs trolley ninety minutes ahead. The corridors of the ward, and the vestibule outside, where the lifts have been coming and going all day, deserted. The voice of the television set in the day room muted at last. Harry lies stretched out, head twisted, mouth open, eyes closed, beak nose to one side, hands on chest – a medieval figure of emaciation and suffering. When he closes his mouth his face is hardly recognisable as a face: it is more like a bag with a single deep crease across it. To look at such a man, at such a moment, is to realise that it is precisely our extraordinary powers of recovery which compel us to suffer and to struggle so greatly before we die. If the struggle goes on intensely enough, or for long enough, however, it begins to look not like a struggle for life but a struggle for death – as if that is the real prize or reward the victor has been seeking and that he will, after making sufficient effort, finally be granted.

Nothing is more difficult to recall, once an experience of hospital life is over, than the sense you have had, while it endured, of its universality. There is no escape from it: not merely no escape for you, there, at that particular moment, but no escape for anyone else either. Everyone has to go through with it: if not now, later; if not in this way, then some other; if not once only, right at the end, then many times and right at the end as well. In a country like England, at any rate, only those who die suddenly or far from all help are spared. To be in the grip of this awareness is like being in the direct presence of birth and death; in comparison, everything you ordinarily busy yourself with shrivels away, reveals as if for ever its frailty and futility. Now you see from what beginnings your life has emerged and to what end it is remorselessly making; now you can judge truthfully the value, or lack of value, of everything that lies between. Surely, you think, such an apprehension will never desert you.

But it will. It has to. That is the condition of your being able to engage once more with the preoccupations, habits, routines, and prepossessions of which your life is for the most part made up. And from *that* perspective, from within the realm of the safe and the quotidian (or of everything that conspires to assure you that you are safe and that your life is well-founded), it is the previous conviction that begins to seem diseased or out of proportion; not a permanent revelation but a symptom merely.

Well, since you do not choose to adopt the one view or the other, but have them both forced on you, each must contain its own truth. To re-create the one truth from the perspective of the other: that is always the task.